FUNDAMENTALS

OF

Seafood Trading

English Language Textbook

First Printing, 2015

ISBN 978-4-908152-06-1

TOEM Publishing
Minami 9, Nishi 7

Sapporo, Japan

064-8561

Notes

Table of Contents

Unit 4

Prices p. 36

Vocabulary: *yen, dollar, pound, euro, yuan, franc*

Listening: Offer Sheet

Reading: Salmon, Sushi, and a Scandanavian Country

Writing: Email to a Buyer

Grammar: Modals (can, will, must...)

Unit 5

Negotiation p. 46

Vocabulary: *negotiate, too high, doesn't make sense, extremely, fair price, expect, take a loss*

Listening: Negotiation

Reading: How to Negotiate in Japan

Writing: Negotiation Quiz

Grammar: Infinitives (to + verb)

Unit 6

Documents p. 54

Vocabulary: *finish, yet, B/L, invoice, origin, certificate, chamber of commerce, attend, confirm*

Listening: Preparing a Shipment

Reading: What is HACCP?

Writing: An Invoice

Grammar: Making Sentences

Unit 7

Inspection p. 62

Vocabulary: *interested in, demand, don't usually, seem, might, find out, reservation, guess*
Listening: Interested in Scallops
Reading: Inspection Process
Writing: Inspection Email
Grammar: Verb tenses

Unit 8

Payment p. 70

Vocabulary: *to be honest, loading, details, offered, I'll get right on it, we can work with that*
Listening: Payment method
Reading: Japanese Prefer Cash to Checks, Cards
Writing: Writing an Invoice
Grammar: Present Tense

Unit 9

Shipping Company p. 78

Vocabulary: *length, width, sent, cartons, height, a shipment of, container, I'll get back to you*
Listening: Shipping Companies
Reading: History of Shipping in Japan
Writing: Past Tense Verbs
Grammar: Past Tense Verbs

Unit 10

Trade Shows p. 86

Vocabulary: *no problem, exhibit, have you, check out, reasonable, sounds good, charge, attend*

Listening: Trade Shows

Reading: Seafood Expo Blog

Writing: Making a Brochure

Grammar: Present Perfect Tense

Dedicated to Hokkaido

The most bountiful island in Japan

Unit 1 First Impressions

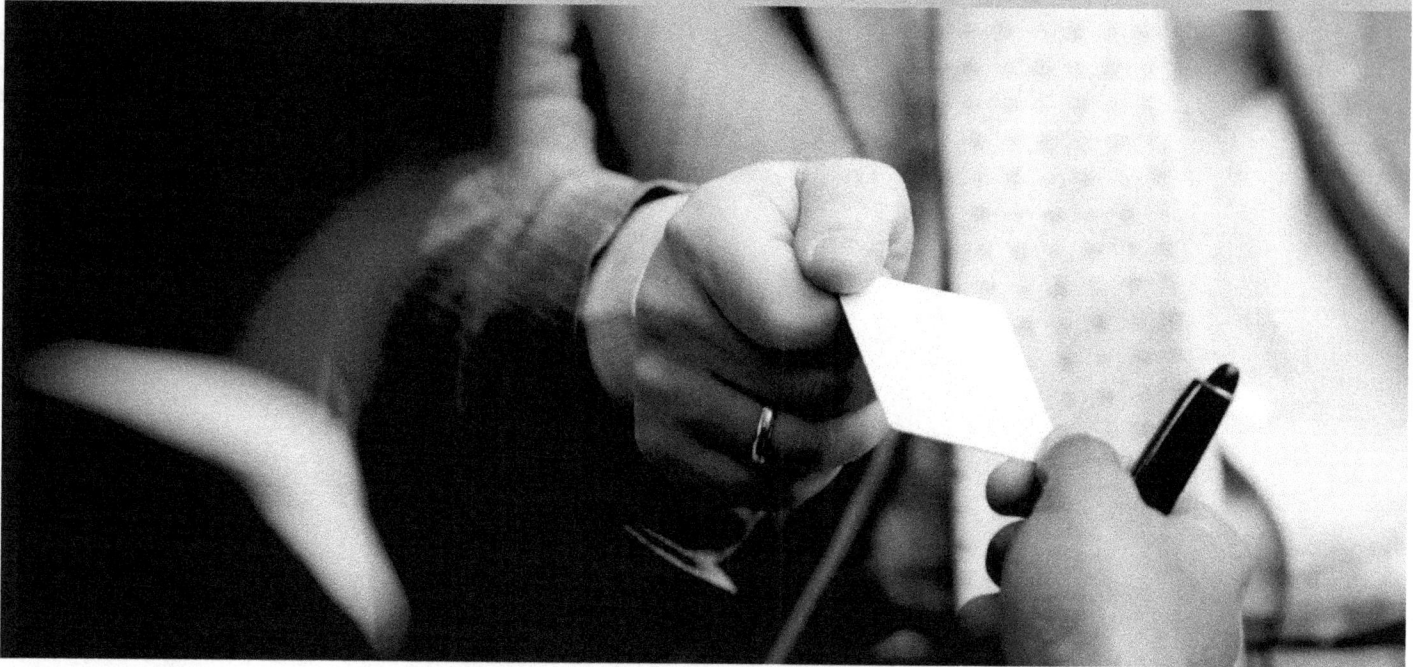

● VOCABULARY

Good morning

Used to

Import

Scallops

About

Stop

Too high

How long have you

Over

Interested in

Mainly

Container

Every 2 months

Always

In demand

Fill in the missing words

1. When I was young, I _____ play baseball every Sunday.

2. What! 10 000¥ for a hot-dog! That's _____ .

3. I brush my teeth for _____ 3 minutes every morning.

4. _____ worked for this company?

5. My friend wants to _____ smoking, but he can't.

6. Western people almost _____ eat bread for breakfast.

7. We have a staff party _____, or 6 times a year.

8. Many foreigners are _____ Japan.

9. Large _____ can be very expensive in restaurants.

10. There are 2 _____ sizes: 20ft and 40ft.

LISTENING PRACTICE

In the dialogue, you will hear two men discussing scallops from Hokkaido. One man is a buyer interested in importing scallops from Japan, and the other works for a seafood trading company in Hokkaido. Listen to the dialogue once, and then answer the questions. After finishing the questions, check your answers.

Questions for Dialogue 1: Brussels Expo

1. When did the buyer stop importing scallops from Hokkaido?

☐ 5 years ago   ☐ 6 years ago   ☐ 7 years ago   ☐ last year

2. What is the main reason the buyer stopped importing scallops?

☐ The distance   ☐ The price   ☐ The quality   ☐ The documents

3. Where is the buyer's company?

☐ Brussels   ☐ Spain   ☐ Sweden   ☐ Japan

4. What sizes does the buyer want?

☐ 3L - 5L   ☐ 3S - 5S   ☐ 1 time every month   ☐ 1 time every 2 months

5. How often does he want to import scallops?

☐ 3L - 5L   ☐ 3S - 5S   ☐ 1 time every month   ☐ 1 time every 2 months

6. How many years has the buyer been in the seafood business?

☐ 20 years   ☐ 7 years   ☐ 1 time every month   ☐ 1 time every 2 months

7. Where is Bill from?

☐ Brussels   ☐ Spain   ☐ Sweden   ☐ Japan

8. When will Nori return to Japan?

☐ In 2 days   ☐ In 2 weeks   ☐ In Hokkaido   ☐ In 3 days

9. What does it mean "secure a supply"?

☐ Ship   ☐ Cook   ☐ Sell   ☐ Get

10. How many Hokkaido scallop companies are able to sell to the EU?

☐ 0   ☐ 1   ☐ 2   ☐ 4

DISCUSSION TOPICS

1. Where would you like to work?

   ☐ A Japanese company   ☐ A foreign company   ☐ Your own company   ☐ The government

2. What does Japan import the most?

   ☐ Wood   ☐ Oil   ☐ Computers   ☐ Alcohol

3. How often do you eat scallops? _____

4. What do you mainly eat for breakfast? _____

5. What products are in demand these days? _____

6. What do you always do when you meet someone? _____

7. How long have you lived in your home? _____

8. What are important to make a good 1st impression (第一印象)?

Arrive early, stay late	Admit mistakes	Don't gossip
Study the company	Be enthusiastic	Finish your work and ask for more
Have confidence	Have lunch with different people	
Go out with co-workers	Share success	

_____

_____

_____

_____

_____

_____

Words to Know

Make a first impression - 第一印象を作る

In the limelight - 脚光を浴びて

Gossip - ゴシップ、噂話

Personal problems - 個人的な問題

Share success - 成功を分かち合う

Enthusiastic - 熱心に

READING - How to Make a Good 1st Impression

In business, it is especially important to make **a good first impression** (感じの良い第一印象を作る). It is important because a good impression can **build trust** (信用を築く). It can start a good relationship with a new customer. When you look good, so does your company. So, meeting new customers well is an important part of business.

Here are some tips to make a good 1st impression, and start a business relationship well.

1) **PREPARE** - Do your homework. Be prepared to meet new customers with knowledge about your business and their business. You will look more professional, confident, and have less **anxiety** (不安).

2) **DRESS WELL** - Make sure your clothes match the situation. Don't be too flashy (派手な) or too casual. Choose clothes that fit and look good. For men, clean shoes, a nice belt and an expensive watch are essentials (不可欠).

3) **LANGUAGE** - It may sound unnecessary, but try to be polite and not use bad words. Being funny can be a great way to make friends, but this is business. Try to **judge the situation** (状況を判断する) when using humor.

4) **HANDSHAKES**: When you shake a man's hand, your handshake should be **firm** (しっかり) and last 2-3 seconds. Look the person in the eye, smile, and say "Nice to meet you".

5) **LISTEN**: Good listeners build trust. Listening allows you to get information and ask **relevant** (適切な) questions. It shows you are interested in what the person is saying. Don't **interrupt** (話を遮る), and let your customer speak.

6) **GOODBYE**: In Japan, we exchange name cards when we meet new people. In Western countries, it is common for people to exchange name cards at the end of a meeting. Asking for a person's business card is a good way to say goodbye. "Let's exchange business cards. I'll contact you as soon as I get home" is a polite way to say goodbye.

READING COMPREHENSION

1. Why is it important to make a good first impression?

_____

2. What are 2 ways people can prepare to meet new customers?

_____

3. Why do you think using too much humor can be bad for business?

_____

4. Which part of the advice on listening do you think is the most useful. Why?

_____

5. In the West, people will sometimes write on business cards. What do you think about this?

_____

WRITING PRACTICE

In this task, students will go into groups of 2 and write a dialogue about a meeting between a buyer and seller. They are meeting for the first time. Put the sentences in the right order.

- Please sit down. Would you like something to drink?
- ~~name is Haruki. Nice to meet you.~~
- No, thank you.
- meet you too. My name is Peter.

- Boiled.
- It's my pleasure to visit you today. This is a very big office.
- Yes, I know about this. These days, I am very interested in importing scallops.
- Are you looking for raw or boiled scallops?
- I want to start with 1 container per month.
- What quantities are you looking for?
- ~~Thank you for coming today. I would like to tell you about our products.~~
- It's a little big, yes. As you know, we export many products, including salmon, crab, and scallops.

- Haruki, that's a great idea. Is 6 okay with you?
- It was very nice meeting you, Peter. By the way, are you free for dinner tonight?

DIALOGUE

Student A (Seller): Hello, my _____ *name is Haruki. Nice to meet you.* _____

Student B (Buyer): It's nice to _____

A: _____

B: _____

A: _____ *Thank you for coming today. I would like to tell you about our products.* _____

B: _____

A: _____

B: _____

C: _____

D: _____

A: _____

B: _____

A: _____

B: _____

GRAMMAR PRACTICE - Adverbs of Frequency

Adverbs of Frequency are used to talk about HOW OFTEN something happens. For example, if you brush your teeth EVERY DAY, you can say, "I **always** brush my teeth." ALWAYS is an adverb of frequency. Here is a list of adverbs of frequency:

Frequency - 周波数

Always (いつも)	100%
Almost always (大抵)	95-99%
Usually (通常)	80%
Often (よく)	80%
Sometimes (時々)	25-75%
Occasionally (時々)	25-75%
Seldom (滅多に...しない)	10-15%
Rarely (まれに)	5%
Almost never (ほとんど...しない)	1-2%
Never (決して)	0%

GRAMMAR TIP

These words can be placed in different places. For example, we can <u>start a sentence </u>with them.

◇ **Sometimes, I wake up late.**

Or <u>before a verb.</u>

◇ **I sometimes wake up late.**

Or <u>at the end </u>of a sentence

◇ **I wake up late sometimes.**

With the BE verb, put the adverb of frequency <u>AFTER the verb</u>, not before.

◇ **I am sometimes tired on Friday.**

Exercise I - Answer the following questions using adverbs of frequency.

1. How often do you eat chocolate for breakfast?

Always	sometimes	never

2. How often do you drink beer at night?

Always	occasionally	rarely

3. How often do you brush your teeth?

Usually	seldom	never

4. Every year, how often do you take a trip?

Almost always	sometimes	seldom

5. How often do you eat scallops?

Occasionally	almost never	never

Exercise II - Answer the following questions. Try to write complete sentences.

1. What do you always do in the morning?

_____

2. What do you never do on Sunday?

_____

3. Do you go to work late?

_____

4. What do you sometimes eat for lunch?

_____

5. Who do you never talk to?

_____

6. When do you take a bath (or shower)?

_____

Answer Key and Notes Unit 1

Vocabulary (p. 10)

1) used to   2) too high   3) about   4) How long have you   5) stop   6) always

7) every 2 months   8) interested in   9) scallops   10) container

Listening (p. 11)

1) 7 years ago   2) the price   3) Spain   4) 3S - 5S   5) 1 time every 2 months

6) 20 years   7) Sweden   8) in 3 days   9) get   10) 2

Reading (p. 13)

Some of these answers are just examples. There are many possible ways to answer questions 3, 5, 6, 7, and 8.

1. A good 1st impression can build trust, and it makes your company look professional and successful.

2. Dress well and be prepared to meet new customers.

3. In my opinion, men should always try to dress neatly. For example, they should try to wear clothes without wrinkles, that fit well, and are appropriate for the situation.

4. Essentials means basic, important, needed.

5. Too much humor might make new customers think you are not professional about your job. They might not want to work with someone who is not serious, especially if they are very serious about their business.

6. I think too much physical contact might make people start to feel uncomfortable.

7. A good listener shows the speaker that he or she is interested in what they are saying.

8. I think every culture is different, and it is important to understand that.

Dialogue: Brussels Expo

A (seller): Hello.
B (buyer/new customer): Good morning.

A: How are you today?
B: Fine thanks. I used to import scallops from Hokkaido about 7 years ago.

A: Why did you stop?
B: The main reason was prices were too high, and it was also really difficult to secure a supply. Some years I could hardly get any scallops at all. My name is Bill.

A: Hello Bill. My name is Nori. Nice to meet you. Where are you from?
B: I'm from Sweden, but my company is in Spain. It is an importing company.

A: How long have you been in the seafood business?
B: Over 20 years. I'm interested in importing Japanese scallops again.

A: What sizes are you looking for?
B: Mainly 3S—5S...about 1 container every 2 months

A: I see. Japanese scallops are some of the best in the world, and those sizes are always in demand.
B: I know. Here is my business card. Let me know if you can do anything.

A: And here is mine. I return to Hokkaido in 3 days. I know there are 2 companies in Hokkaido that can supply the EU market. When I get back, I will contact them and get back to you with some information.
B: Nori, nice to meet you. Have a safe trip back.

A: Same to you, Bill. Very nice meeting you.

Writing (p. 14)

Student A (Seller): Hello, my name is Peter.

Student B (Buyer): It's nice to meet you Peter. My name is Alan.

A: Have you ever tried our pasta sauce?

B: Peter, I love this product and I am interested in importing it.

A: I agree it's a great product. Have you ever imported it before?

B: About 10 years ago, but I want to start again. Have you ever shipped to Spain?

A: Around 6 months ago, we sent a shipment to France. 9 tons.

B: Do you remember the cost of the freight and documents?

C: At the moment I don't. But let me take your contact information, and I'll get back to you.

D: Here's my business card. I'm interested in one container every 2 months. I already have buyers waiting. Can you handle this?

A: If it's a 20ft container, no problem.

B: To start, that's exactly what I want.

A: Alan, it was great meeting you. When I get back home, I'll contact you with that information.

B: Peter, the pleasure was mine. Looking forward to working with you sonn. Thanks. Bye.

Notes

Unit 2 - Gathering Information

VOCABULARY

Match the English words with the Japanese words. Which word doesn't have a match?

1. Who	a) 誰の
2. How many	b) なぜ
3. What kind of	c) どんな
4. How long does it take	d) どこに
5. Whose	e) 幾つ
6. Where	f) それはどのくらいかかりますか
7. How often	g) どのくらいの頻度で
8. How much	h) どちら
9. When	i) どの位
10. Why	j) いつ
11. Which	k) 誰が

20

LISTENING PRACTICE

In the dialogue, you will hear two men discussing the trade show Nori went to. Listen to the dialogue once, and then answer the questions. After finishing the questions, check your answers. Listen to the dialogue a second time to check your answers one more time.

Questions for Dialogue 2: Meeting with the Boss

1. When did Nori arrive in Japan?

   ☐ At 9pm   ☐ At 10pm   ☐ At 11pm   ☐ At midnight

2. How many name cards did Nori receive?

   ☐ Exactly 120   ☐ Under 130   ☐ Over 130   ☐ Yes, he did

3. Where are the countries located?

   ☐ Mainly in Asia ☐ Mainly in Africa ☐ Mainly America   ☐ Mainly Europe

4. When is Nori free?

   ☐ At 9 o'clock   ☐ At 10 o'clock   ☐ At 10: 30   ☐ At 11 o'clock

5. Who will Nori meet?

   ☐ Nissui owner   ☐ Nissui rep   ☐ Asian buyer   ☐ American buyer

6. What will Nori and the person he is meeting talk about?

   ☐ Trip to Brussels ☐ Business cards   ☐ Japanese companies ☐ Routes & prices

7. What will Nori and the boss discuss?

   ☐ Trip to Brussels ☐ Business cards   ☐ Japanese companies ☐ Routes & prices

8. Where will Nori and the boss meet?

   ☐ In Brussels   ☐ At 10 o'clock   ☐ After the meeting ☐ Boss' office

9. How many Japanese companies attended the trade show?

   ☐ Plenty   ☐ A great deal   ☐ Hardly any   ☐ None

10. What is Nori's boss' name?

   ☐ Mr. Muto   ☐ Mr. Suzuki   ☐ Mr. Okuyama   ☐ Mr. Sato

DISCUSSION TOPICS

1. How many times have you been to a foreign country?

    _____

2. How long does it take you to go to your job (or school)?

    _____

3. How often do you have a meeting?

    _____

4. Where were you born?

    _____

5. When was the last time you ate at a restaurant?

    _____

6. How much does your bag cost?

    _____

7. What do you think are good qualities of a boss?

☐ Help workers	☐ Have big dreams	☐ Take chances to grow the company
☐ Be a good motivator	☐ Act professional	☐ Act emotional
☐ Protect workers	☐ Have clear goals	☐ Much work experience
☐ Good sense of humor	☐ Give useful advice	☐ Be handsome/beautiful

8. Is it better to be a worker or a boss? Why? _____

    _____

    _____

    _____

    _____

Words to Know

Sense of humor - ユーモアがある

Give advice - アドバイスする

Motivate - やる気にさせる

L/C - buyer's bank promises seller's bank to make payment

Take chances - 勝負に出る

Emotional - 感情の

When was the last time - 前回はいつでしたか？

READING - Company Profiles

Trading with foreign companies can be risky: Communication problems, different banking systems, long distance shipping, to name a few. However, one way to **reduce** (減らす) this risk is by exchanging information with a trading partner. And it is best to do this before any contracts are signed.

Many Japanese companies show their profiles openly online. This is not true with foreign companies. I have received some unfriendly emails from customers who don't want to share this information. Here is an email from one foreign buyer not wanting to share information with a Japanese supplier:

> I am not sure why you need our company outline. This is the first time a supplier asks for this info. There is some info that we don't want to **disclose** (開示する). All of our purchases are paid by L/C within 5 days after the product passes **inspection** (検査を通過する).

Company profiles are useful for many reasons. They give the seller an idea of whether the buying company can make a **suitable** (条件に見合う) trading partner. Company profiles include years in business, banks used, and most importantly, the payment method. The safest payment method for the seller is a cash payment before the products are moved from storage. As the **relationship** (関係) between companies grows, friendlier payment methods for the buyer can usually be reached.

For some companies, international trade can be very **profitable** (有益). An example of this is Toyota Motors, which earns the majority of its profits from international sales. In 2014, Toyota became the first Japanese company to earn over 2 trillion yen (2 兆円).

All businesses want to have partners they can trust. In order to build trust, partners need to share information with each other to better understand one another. A company profile is an **effective** (効果的な) way to start building a trusting relationship.

READING COMPREHENSION

1. How can companies develop a trusting relationship?

_____

2. What kind of information is in a company profile?

_____

3. Why do you think the foreign buyer was upset?

_____

4. For a seller, what is the best payment method?

_____

5. What do you think is the most difficult part of international trade?

_____

Su Shin Fishery Enterprise

1. 会社名: Su Shin Fishery Enterprise Co., Ltd

2. 所在地: 2F, No. 17, Chienkang Rd., Jhonghe City, Taipei County 255 (Exit at Jhonghe Interchange) – Registered Office.

3. 創 立: 1960

4. 代表者: Hua Tai Jung

5. 資本金: US$3,750,000

6. 従業員数: 130 名

7. 売上高:(毎年): US$25,500,000 (2012)

8. 取引銀行: HSBC, Chang Hwa Commercial Bank Ltd., etc.

9. 取引先: 主な取引先国 中国、日本、東南アジア諸国、ヨーロッパ諸国, 中央アメリカ諸国など

10. 主な事業内容: 世界中から水産物や、水産加工品の輸入を行い、台湾国内に流通業、販売業を行っています。

11. 連絡先 – Liv Lee, Email: liv.lee@sushinfishery.com.tw Phone: +886 817 4722 Ext 66.

12. 支払方法: L/C

Su Shin Fishery Enterprise

1. _____: Su Shin Fishery Enterprise Co., Ltd

2. _____: 2F, No. 17, Chienkang Rd., Jhonghe City, Taipei County 255

3. _____: 1960

4. _____: Hua Tai Jung

5. _____: US$3,750,000

6. _____: 130名

7. _____: US$25,500,000 (2012)

8. _____: HSBC, Chang Hwa Commercial Bank Ltd., etc.

9. _____:

_____

10. _____:

_____

11. _____: Liv Lee, Email: liv.lee@sushinfishery.com.tw Phone: +886 817 4722

12. _____: L/C

GRAMMAR PRACTICE - Time Words

In the dialogue and the reading sections in unit 2, we can read and hear time words used a lot. 'Before signing a contract', 'last night', 'in 30 minutes', and 'after the meeting' are some of the time words used in this unit.

Time words tell us which verb tenses to use, and they tell us how actions are connected. Here is a short list of time words:

Past Tense - Yesterday, Last week, Two days ago, Once upon a time, In the past, When I was _____ (young, 17 years old...)

Present Tense - Right now, Every day, At the moment, These days, Recently, Nowadays

Future Tense - Tomorrow, Next month, In 3 hours, One day, In the future, Soon, In a while

Another group of time words is called Adverb Clauses of Time. They show the relationship between actions.

Here is a short list:

• When	• The next time	• Until
• While	• The last time	• Whenever
• After	• As soon as	• Every time
• Before	• Since	
• The first time	• For	

Finish the sentences below using the correct TIME WORD. There are many possible answers.

1. _____, I am using my computer.

2. It is 3pm right now. _____, it will be 5pm.

3. I have had my car _____ I moved to this city.

4. _____ I saw you, I thought you were very nice.

5. _____, dinosaurs lived in China.

6. _____ I come here, I always eat breakfast at home.

7. _____ I was driving here, I saw a cute lady riding her bike.

8. I eat bread _____.

9. This year, I went to Hawaii. _____, I want to go to Hong Kong.

10. _____ I wake up, I always drink water.

Answer Key and Notes Unit 2

Vocabulary (p. 20)

1. no match   2. E   3. C   4. F   5. A   6. D   7. G   8. I   9. J   10. B   11. H

Listening (p. 21)

1. 10 pm	4. After 10:30	7. The trip to Brussels	10. Mr. Sato
2. Over 130	5. Nissui shipping rep	8. In the boss' office	
3. Mainly from Asia	6. Shipping routes and prices	9. Hardly any	

Reading (p. 22)

1. They can exchange information

2. Years in business, banks used, and payment method

3. FOR EXAMPLE - *It is not the custom to exchange information in other countries*

4. Cash before loading

5. FOR EXAMPLE - *Visiting each other or establishing a personal relationship*

6. FOR EXAMPLE - *Toyota makes an excellent product*

7. FOR EXAMPLE - *Cultural differences*

Writing (p. 24)

(1) **Name of the company** – Su Shin Fishery Enterprise Co., Ltd

(2) **Location** – 2F, No. 17, Chienkang Rd., Jhonghe City, Taipei County 255 (Exit at Jhonghe Interchange) – Registered Office.

(3) **Date Founded** - 1960

(4) **President** - Hua Tai Jung

(5) **Paid-up Capital** - US$3,750,000

(6) **Number of Employees** - 130

(7) **Sales** (Yearly) - US$25,500,000 (2012)

(8) **Banks Used** - HSBC, Chang Hwa Commercial Bank Ltd., etc.

(9) **Foreign Countries Working In** - Importing raw materials or finished products from around the world: China, Japan, South East Asia, Europe, Central America, etc.

(10) **Main Activities:** Importing raw materials worldwide and reprocessing them in our own factory and distributing the finished products domestically. Importing marine products worldwide for wholesalers, chain stores, and traditional markets.

(11) **Contact info** – Liv Lee, Email: liv.lee@sushinfishery.com.tw Phone: +886 817 4722

(12) **Payment Method** - L/C

Grammar (p. 2)

1. right now   2. after 2 hours   3. since   4. the first time   5. once upon a time

6. before   7. while   8. every day   9. next year   10. as soon as

Dialogue

Boss: Hi Nori, when did you get back from Brussels?

Nori: Hello Mr. Sato. I got back last night around 10pm.

B: So, how was the trade show?

N: I met many buyers, and many of them are interested in working with us.

B: How many name cards did you get?

N: Just over 130.

B: Excellent. Where are these companies located?

N: Mainly in Asia, but a few from the USA, France and Spain.

B: Were there many Japanese companies at the trade show?

N: Hardly any.

B: Make a list of the companies, and let's discuss your trip. It's 10 o'clock now. When are you free?

N: I have a meeting in 30 minutes. After that, I have time to meet.

B: Who are you meeting?

N: The shipping rep from Nissui. He wants to talk about new routes and prices.

B: Okay, let's meet in my office after your meeting.

Unit 3 - Products Available

Can you name thee types of catching/growing methods?

Write the answers with the correct picture: *troller*, *purse seiner*, *trawler*, *gill net*

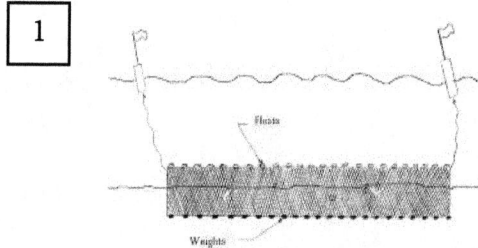

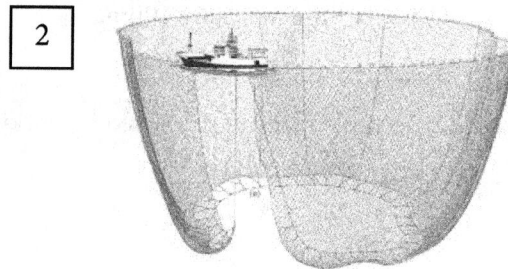

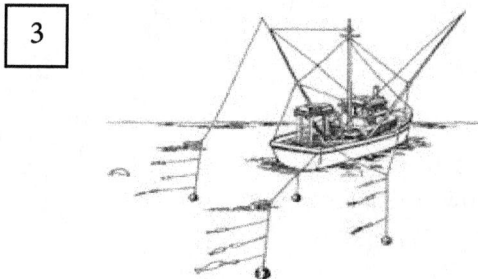

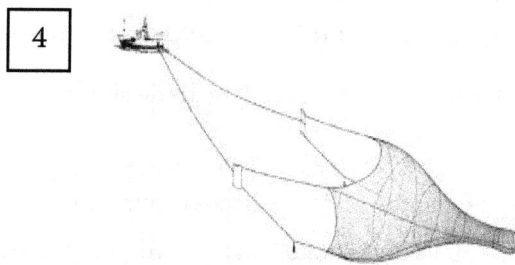

1

2

3

4

● VOCABULARY

Match the words to their meaning

1. Work with	a) 99%
2. Flight	b) Get ready for
3. Look over	c) Doing
4. Almost all	d) Give
5. Products	e) Airplane trip
6. Catch schedule	f) Do something together
7. Prepare	g) Things a company sells
8. Handed	h) Check
9. While	i) During that time
10. HACCP	j) Time fishermen get fish
11. Working on	k) Hazard Analysis and Critical Control Points

LISTENING PRACTICE

In the dialogue, you will hear two men discussing the business people Nori met in Brussels. After finishing the questions, check your answers. Listen to the dialogue a second time to check your answers one more time.

Questions for Dialogue 3: Products Available for Export

1. When did Nori look over his notes about the companies?

   ☐ At the hotel   ☐ On the plane   ☐ In Japan   ☐ At the office

2. How many companies does Nori think are a good match for his company?

   ☐ 10   ☐ 12   ☐ 14   ☐ 15

3. Why does Nori think the companies are good?

   ☐ Want their products   ☐ Have much money   ☐ King crab & shrimp   ☐ Met in Brussel

4. What did Nori prepare before going to Brussels?

   ☐ Catch schedule   ☐ Gifts   ☐ HACCP   ☐ The customers

5. After Nori handed the information to the buyers, they looked more

   ☐ Interested   ☐ Tired   ☐ Excited   ☐ Angry

6. What did Sato san buy while Nori was gone?

   ☐ Squid & shrimp   ☐ Tuna & Hokke   ☐ Crab & Salmon   ☐ King crab & cod

7. What do you think H&G means?

   ☐ Heart & guts   ☐ Head & Guts   ☐ Hokkaido & Guam   ☐ Heat & Grill

8. How much king crab did Sato san buy?

   ☐ 10t   ☐ 20t   ☐ 30t   ☐ 40t

9. Where is the king crab from?

   ☐ Brussels   ☐ Canada   ☐ Russia   ☐ Alaska

10. Does the salmon have HACCP?

   ☐ Yes, it can   ☐ Yes, it will   ☐ No, it doesn't   ☐ No, it didn't

DISCUSSION TOPICS

1. Where do you eat seafood, at home or at a restaurant?

2. Is there any food that you don't like to eat?

3. When you buy or eat fish, what is important to you (price, freshness, kind of fish, season...)?

4. Tuna is an expensive fish. Why do some people pay so much money for 1 fish?

5. If you were a fish, what kind would it be, and where would you like to live?

6. How do you like to eat seafood?

7. What seafood does Japan export?

8. How do you feel about farmed fish?

_____

_____

_____

_____

_____

_____

_____

IN SEASON?

Read the list of seafood below, and decide what season or seasons (spring, summer, fall, or winter) the seafood is caught in the largest seafood catching are in Japan: Hokkaido.

		Spring	Summer	Fall/Autumn	Winter
1.	Large sized scallops (M, L, 2L...)	☐	☐	☐	☐
2.	Boiled scallops	☐	☐	☐	☐
3.	Chum salmon	☐	☐	☐	☐
4.	Hair crab	☐	☐	☐	☐
5.	Pacific saury	☐	☐	☐	☐
6.	Yellowtail	☐	☐	☐	☐
7.	Hokke	☐	☐	☐	☐
8.	Yellow rock fish	☐	☐	☐	☐
9.	Buri	☐	☐	☐	☐
10.	Kinki	☐	☐	☐	☐

READING - How Bluefin Tuna Became a Million-Dollar Fish

On the first Saturday of the year, there is a tuna auction at Tsukiji market. Almost every year, one person pays a lot of money for a tuna. And for several years, that person was Kiyoshi Kimura.

In 2012, Mr. Kimura paid a lot of money for 1 bluefin tuna. He spent $736,000 (USD), and he was the 1st person to buy a tuna that year. In 2013, Mr. Kimura paid even more money. He spent 1.76 million dollars to buy the first bluefin tuna that year. The fish **weighed** (重さが...である) 221.8kg. But 2014 was different. Mr. Kimura bought the first tuna, but he paid only $70,000. In 2015, he paid just over $40 000.

That's still a lot of money for bluefin tuna in Japan. But many people were waiting for Mr. Kimura to pay an exorbitant amount of money. In 2014 and 2015, compared to other years, the prices were very cheap.

Why does Mr. Kimura pay a lot of money for the 1st bluefin tuna of the year? Is it because bluefin tuna is very, very **rare** (貴重)? Is bluefin tuna so delicious that people pay a lot of money to eat it? Is Mr. Kimura **insane** (非常識)?

Some people think the tuna market is out ofcontrol. Some people think buyers spend high prices for a fish that is disappearing from our oceans. But this is not exactly true.

At Tsukiji, it is an honor to buy the first tuna of the year. Mr. Kimura gets free advertising for doing this. His name and restaurant are in newspapers and on TV in Japan and around the world. It also shows his **competitors** (競合他社) that he is rich and can spend a lot of money for his business.

In the 1970s, bluefin tuna started to become very popular in sushi restaurants. In the 1960s, nobody wanted to eat the fatty fish, and it was used for cat food. But between 1970 and 1990, fishing for bluefin increased by 2000%.

Demand for bluefin in Japan is high. Markets across Japan auction tuna every morning. Buyers pay a great deal of money to buy tuna, and it is one of the most expensive wild animals in the world.

The bluefin tuna is a rare fish. It is not easy to find it in the **wild** (天然), and in the future, nobody knows if there will be any bluefin left in the oceans for Mr. Kimura to buy.

READING COMPREHENSION

1. When is the 1st tuna of the year sold?

_____

2. Why does Mr. Kimura buy this fish?

_____

3. How do you think it tastes?

_____

4. Why do you think bluefin tuna was not so popular in Japan before the 1970s?

_____

5. Why do you think Mr. Kimura paid 'only' $40,000 for the tuna in 2015?

_____

WRITING PRACTICE - Charts and the writing activity

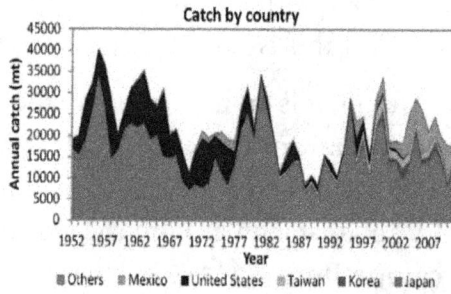

Catch by country

Figure 1. Historical annual catch of Pacific bluefin tuna by country, 1952-2011(data in calendar year 1952 and 2010 are incomplete).

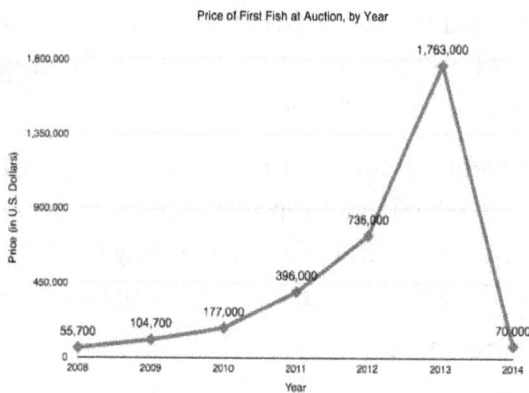

Price of First Fish at Auction, by Year

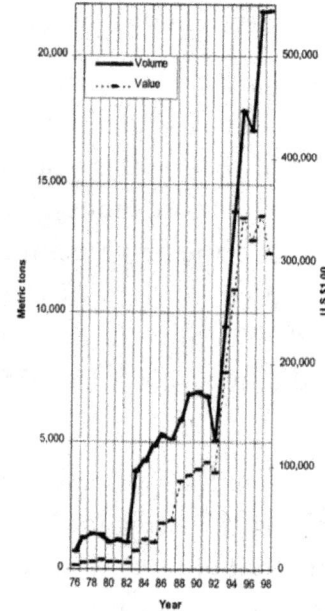

Figure 12. Japanese imports of fresh and frozen bluefin tuna, 1976-1998. (Source: Japan Marine Products Importers Association 1977-1999)

Use the charts above to complete the writing about the world tuna market.

(1) _____ the 1970s, only _____ and _____ and caught a lot of bluefin tuna. However, other _____ and such as Korea and _____ and started to fish for bluefin. In 2007, Mexico was the _____ and biggest catcher in the world. (2) _____ and 1976 _____ and 1998, the number of bluefin being caught _____ very much. In 1976, about 20 metric tons of bluefin was caught, but in 1998, _____ 20,000 metric tons was caught. (3) _____, one person paid $55,700 for the 1st bluefin of the year. Recently, the _____ price paid was $1,763,000 by Mr. Kimura.

32

Answer Key and Notes Unit 3

Types of Catch/Growing Methods (p. 28)

1. Gill net   2. Purse seiner   3. Troller   4. Trawler

Vocabulary (p. 28)

1. F   2. E   3. H   4. A   5. G   6. J   7. B   8. D   9. I   10. K   11. C

Listening Practice (p. 29)

1. On the plane   3. Want their products   5. Interested   7. Head & Guts   9. Alaska

2. 15   4. Catch schedule   6. Crab & Salmon   8. 20t   10. No, it doesn't

Discussion: In Season? (p. 30)

1. Hotate - Winter & spring   5. Sanma - Fall   9. Buri - Winter

2. Boiled hotate - All year   6. Hamachi - Winter   10. Kinki - All year

3. Sake - Fall & winter   7. Hokke - All year

4. Kegani - Spring   8. Yanagi nomai - Summer

Reading (p.31)

1. On the 1st Saturday in January.

2. It is good for his business.

3. I think it doesn't taste so good because it is old.

4. Maybe people thought it had too much fat.

5. Maybe his competitors had no money.

Writing Practice (p.32)

Some of these answers are suggestions. There can be many different answers.

(1) BEFORE the 1970s, only JAPAN and THE USA caught bluefin tuna. However, other countries such as Korea and MEXICO started to fish for bluefin. In 2007, Mexico was the SECOND biggest catcher in the world. (2) FROM 1976 TO 1998, the number of bluefin being caught INCREASED very much. In 1976, about 20 metric tons of bluefin was caught, but in 1998, ABOUT/AROUND/CLOSE TO/OVER 20,000 metric tons was caught. (3) IN 2008, one person paid $55,700 for the 1st bluefin of the year. Recently, the HIGHEST/BIGGEST price paid was $1,763,000 by Mr. Kimura.

Dialogue - Products Available for Export

Sato san: You met many buyers in Brussels. Which companies do you think we can work with?
Nori san: On the flight back, I looked over everything, and I think there are about 15 companies we can work with.

Sato: What do they want to import?
Nori: They all asked for products we have...scallops, salmon, squid, shrimp, hair crab...

Sato: It was smart of you to prepare a catch schedule and list of products available before you left.
Nori: I thought it might be useful. After I handed them the information, they seemed more interested.

Sato: Okay, while you were gone, we bought king crab and salmon. The salmon is chum, product of Hokkaido, H&G. The crab is product of Alaska, 900g up sections. We purchased 20t.
Nori: Have you set a price, and do you have the sizes for the salmon?

Sato: I'm working on the prices now. Here are the salmon sizes (hands Nori a piece of paper).
Nori: Does the salmon have HACCP?

Sato: No, it doesn't.

Notes

Unit 4 - Prices

Currencies - *Below is a list of the world's most used currencies. What are their names, and which are the most popular?*

1. ___British Pound Sterling___

2. _____

3. _____

4. _____

5. _____

6. _____

7. _____

8. _____

9. _____

10. _____

11. _____

12. ___Hong Kong Dollar___

LISTENING PRACTICE

In the dialogue, Sato san and Nori san discuss selling salmon and king crab to foreign buyers. Listen to the dialogue once, and then answer the questions. After finishing the questions, check your answers. Listen to the dialogue a second time to check your answers one more time.

Questions for Dialogue 4: Offer Sheet

1. What will Nori try to sell?

   ☐ Scallops & salmon   ☐ Squid & salmon   ☐ King crab & salmon   ☐ Scallops

2. Where is the foreign company based?

   ☐ Hong Kong   ☐ Brussels   ☐ Hokkaido   ☐ Tokyo

3. When will Sato san's company have scallops?

   ☐ In a while   ☐ Next year   ☐ In the past   ☐ Soon

4. What is the name of the shipping company?

   ☐ Mitsui   ☐ Nissui   ☐ Kawasaki   ☐ Nippon Yusen

5. How much did the company pay for the salmon per kilo?

   ☐ 300 ¥   ☐ 400 ¥   ☐ 420 ¥   ☐ 500 ¥

6. Why is salmon so expensive this year?

   ☐ Increased demand   ☐ Fewer fishermen   ☐ Out of season   ☐ Fewer fish

7. What does Nori's girlfriend love to eat?

   ☐ Salmon   ☐ Scallops   ☐ Shopping   ☐ Salmon roe

8. What do you think 'sub-con offer' means?

   ☐ Cash only offer   ☐ Not firm offer   ☐ Time limit offer   ☐ Firm offer

9. How much profit does the company make per kilogram?

   ☐ 20 ¥   ☐ 400 ¥   ☐ 25 ¥   ☐ 500 ¥

10. Why is it easier to work with Hong Kong buyers?

   ☐ Distance   ☐ Documents   ☐ Language   ☐ Demand

DISCUSSION TOPICS

1. How do you say these numbers?

   400: _____ 515/kg: _____ 10,000: _____

   340,000: _____ 17,000,000: _____

2. How much did you pay for your shoes? _____

3. If you send a package, which company do you use? _____

4. Do you think 5% profit is a fair number? _____

5. What kinds of documents do you think are needed to export? _____

6. What kind of expensive foods or drinks have you tried? _____

7. Shipping Lines are companies that own ships. They are important to the world economy, and they get special privileges (特権). Which of these are true?

   ☐ Can delay your shipment   ☐ Can throw your shipment into the ocean   ☐ Can sell your shipment for gas

   ☐ Get paid before releasing the shipment   ☐ Can change your schedule   ☐ Pay nothing for damaged shipments

8. Is it good to have a strong or weak yen? Why and why not?

   _____

   _____

   _____

   _____

Words to Know

Offer sheet - 見積書

Based in - に基づく

At the moment - 現時点では

Soon - すぐに

Prepare - 準備する

H&G - ヘッドレス

Release - 手放す

The catch is down - 不漁

Is like - 〜のような

Sub-con offer - 買手が承諾しても売手の最終確認があって、初めて契約が成立するOFFERのこと。

Of course - もちろん

Right away - 直ちに

Damaged - 傷ついた

READING - Salmon, Sushi, and a Scandinavian Country

Before the 1970s, Japanese people did not eat salmon sushi. And Japan did not import a lot of fish. Things have changed very much in Japan.

In the early 1970s, Japan caught **enough** (十分な) fish to feed all of its people. At that time, each Japanese person ate about 60kg of seafood every year. Japanese fishermen could export seafood at that time.

In the mid-1990s, this changed. Japan did not catch enough fish, collecting about 50% of the seafood needed to supply the **demand** (需要を満たす) from Japanese consumers. There were 2 main reasons for this change.

The first was **overfishing** (乱獲). There was no quota system in Japan at that time. The second reason was the exclusive economic zone (EEZ). The EEZ is a 200 mile zone, and it **sets** (決める) a country's water borders. In 1996, Japan started to follow the EEZ. This **limited** (限られた) Japanese fishermen to areas within the Japanese zone.

In 1974, Thor Listau visited Japan. He was in the Norwegian government, and he realized Japan was an excellent market for Norwegian fish. In 1985, he started Project Japan. Its **goal** (目標) was to promote the Norwegian seafood industry in Japan.

In 1985, Norway exported over 30,000,000¥ of seafood products. This was about 1% of Japan's total imports of seafood. In 1991, exports to Japan increased to ¥90,000,000, and this was changing how Japanese people ate salmon. At that time, people preferred tuna or sea bream for raw dishes. Salmon was grilled or used for *kirimi*. People thought salmon was dangerous to eat raw because of **parasites** (寄生虫).

But Thor Listau did not give up. "We had to fight to introduce salmon into the market," says Mr. Listau. It took 15 years, but in 1995, salmon used for sushi became popular. For salmon to become popular as sushi, Norwegian workers at Project Japan talked with Japanese importers, supermarket chains, stores, restaurants, and the Norwegian **ambassador** (大使) served salmon to all his guests.

Success in Japan led to success in other Asian countries. In 2011, Norway exported more salmon to China than to Japan. Almost all of it was eaten raw.

READING COMPREHENSION

1. What do you think hurt the seafood industry in Japan more, overfishing or the EEZ? Why?

_____

2. Why didn't people like to eat raw salmon?

_____

3. How did Norwegians get people in Japan to start eating raw salmon?

_____

4. Why is Japan seen as an important market?

_____

5. How long did it take Project Japan to have success?

_____

WRITING PRACTICE- Email To Buyer

With the information below, write an email to a foreign buyer in Hong Kong. You want "Jason" to buy your product. You met Jason at a trade show in Tokyo 3 months ago. You are selling frozen, boiled king crab, product of Russia. Use the information below to write the email. Be sure to have an introduction (Dear Jason) and departing remark (Best regards, your name). It is important to write short, concise emails, so only use the space available on this page for your email.

- Product - King crab (frozen, boiled)
- Size - 5L
- Number of products - approx. 2 sections/carton
- Net weight - 3kg/carton
- C&F Hong Kong price - ¥ 3,700/kg

- Country of origin - Russia
- Offer deadline—October 27
- Price includes 3 documents - invoice, packing list, and B/L
- Minumum order - 9t

From:	
To:	
Cc:	
Sent:	
Subject:	

GRAMMAR PRACTICE - Modals (助動詞)

In the reading Salmon, Sushi, and a Scandanavian Country, there are many examples of modals. We read that Japanese people DID not EAT salmon raw, and Norwegians COULD EXPORT more and more salmon to Japan. Did and Could are 2 modals.

RULES

Modal + verb (no TO) - I will eat bread tonight (NOT I <u>will to eat</u> bread tonight)

Modal + NOT + Verb for negatives - I do not like tests

Modals don't use S for 3rd person - He can play (no S)

Modals are used in many ways. **May/Might** show possibility (可能性). **Must/Have to/Had to/Be supposed to/Had better** show obligation (義務). **May I/Can I** ask for permission (きよか). **Can/Be able to** show ability (能力). **Will/Be going to** show the future (未来), and **should** is used for suggestions (提案)

Exercise I - Match the words with the correct Japanese word

1. can _____   4. did _____   7. had to _____   10. may _____

2. might _____   5. must _____   8. am supposed to _____

3. will _____   6. should _____   9. had better _____

A. ～かも知れない	D. ～すべきである	G. ～した方が良い	J. ～できる
B. ～する予定	E. ～しなければならない	H. ～した	
C. ～する事になっている	F. ～しなければならない	I. ～かも知れない	

Exercise II - Choose the right answer for each sentence.

1. He _____ speak French. He lived in Paris for 3 years.

   ☐ will   ☐ can   ☐ did

2. What _____ you do tomorrow?

   ☐ might   ☐ will   ☐ should

3. You _____ stop smoking. It's bad for your health.

   ☐ had to   ☐ will   ☐ should

4. Yesterday, I _____ take a test. It was hard.

   ☐ may   ☐ should   ☐ did

5. It's a little cloudy. I think it _____ rain today.

   ☐ had better   ☐ will   ☐ had to

Exercise III - Answer the following questions. Try to write complete sentences.

1. What did you have to do yesterday?

_____

2. What won't you do next week?

_____

3. What might you do this weekend?

_____

4. What country don't you want to visit?

_____

5. What couldn't you do yesterday?

_____

Answer Key and Notes Unit 4

Vocabulary (p. 36)

1. UK pound sterling

2. European euro

3. Canadian dollar

4. Australian dollar

5. Chinese yuan

6. Thai baht

7. US dollar

8. Japanese yen

9. Taiwan dollar

10. Swiss franc

11. Korean won

12. Hong Kong dollar

Listening (p. 37)

1. Salmon & king crab

2. Hong Kong

3. Soon

4. Nissui

5. 400¥

6. Fewer fish

7. Salmon roe

8. Not firm offer

9. 20¥

10. Documents

Discussion Topics (p. 38)

1. **400** - 4 hundred   **515/kg** - 5 hundred and fifteen PER kilogram   **10,000** - 10 thousand
340,000 - 3 hundred and 40 thousand   **17,000,000** - 17 million

5. An invoice, packing list, bill of lading and country of origin are needed for exporting products. Other documents may include a health cetificate and a radiation certificate. For health certificates, the seller should confirm what needs to be looked for (i.e. DSP [下痢性貝中毒], Escherichia coli [大腸菌])

7. Shipping Lines can't sell your goods for gas. Everything else is true.

Reading (p. 39)

1. Open answer
2. Too dangerous to eat
3. Started Project Japan and spoke to many people in the seafood industry
4. Success in Japan can lead to success in Asia
5. 15 years

Writing (p. 40) - Email to Hong Kong buyer

Dear Jason,

It was a pleasure meeting you in Tokyo. I have an offer for frozen bolied king crab. The size is 5L, product of Russia. The product is sold in 3kg cartons, approximately 2 sections per carton. The minimum order is 9t. For a 9t order, the C&F price (Hong Kong) is 3,700¥ /kg. This offer is good until October 27 (year).

If interested, please let me know.

Best regards,

(your name)

Grammar (p.41) - Exercise I

1. J	3. C	5. E	7. B	9. G
2. A	4. H	6. D	8. F	10. I

Grammar (p.41) - Exercise II

1. Can   2. will   3. should   4. had to   5. may

Dialogue— Offer Sheet

Sato: Nori, contact the buyers you met in Brussels. Write an offer sheet for the salmon and king crab.
Nori: One buyer asked about Hokkaido salmon...and scallops. The company is based in Hong Kong.

Sato: We don't have scallops at the moment, but we will soon.
Nori: Okay, I'll prepare an offer sheet for the salmon, and try to sell the king crab as well.

Sato: Use Mr. Sakuma at Nissui Transportation for the shipping.
Nori: We bought the salmon at 400 yen per kilogram, frozen H&G, right?

Sato: I told you this before. Yes.
Nori: It's expensive this year.

Sato: The catch is down about 30%. Salmon roe is like gold this year.
Nori: And my girlfriend loves ikura...arrrr.

Sato: Go fishing. Anyways, add 20 yen per kg to the cost, plus mention that this is a sub-con offer.
Nori: Hong Kong buyers don't usually ask for any special documents, so it's easier to work with them.

Sato: Ask anyways, okay?
Nori: Of course, I'll do that right away.

Notes

Unit 5 - Negotiations

VOCABULARY

Negotiate

Just a moment

The price is too high

Doesn't make sense

Extremely

Mention

Fair price

Take a loss

Purchase

Expect

Finish the sentences with the correct word

1. In Canada, the weather can be _____ cold.

2. I _____ the price of gold will go down.

3. He wants to buy a house in the future, but _____.

4. He doesn't like the price, so we will _____.

5. I have to ask my boss something. _____ please.

6. What! The deal is canceled? That _____.

7. I would like to _____ 9t of frozen hair crab.

LISTENING PRACTICE

In this dialogue, Nori contacts Jason, the Hong Kong buyer. The buyer is not happy about the price of the salmon. Listen to the dialogue once, and then answer the questions. After finishing the questions, check your answers. Listen to the dialogue a second time to check your answers one more time.

Questions for Dialogue 5: Negotiation

1. Why is Jason not interested in the salmon?

   ☐ Quality   ☐ Price   ☐ Shipping   ☐ Demand

2. What price could Jason pay for the Canadian salmon?

   ☐ 250 yen   ☐ 260 yen   ☐ 350 yen   ☐ 360 yen

3. Do you think Jason knew the salmon was *mejika* chum salmon?

   ☐ No, I can't   ☐ No, I don't   ☐ No, I won't   ☐ No, I didn't

4. What is special about *mejika* salmon?

   ☐ Good quality   ☐ Good name   ☐ Good price   ☐ Good size

5. How much cheaper is the king crab compared to prices in Hong Kong?

   ☐ 10% cheaper   ☐ Same price   ☐ 15% cheaper   ☐ 5% cheaper

6. What does Jason mean when he says "I will take a loss on the salmon"?

   ☐ Make money   ☐ Lose money   ☐ Can't find money   ☐ Spend money

7. What is Jason's family name?

   ☐ Tsui   ☐ Wang   ☐ Zhang   ☐ Li

8. What does Jason ask Nori to send him?

   ☐ Photos & samples   ☐ Scallops   ☐ Sizes & prices   ☐ Salmon

9. Nori's company is purchasing a _____ amount of scallops.

   ☐ Good   ☐ Small   ☐ Large   ☐ Delicious

10. Nori tells Jason he will contact him _____.

    ☐ First   ☐ Second   ☐ Third   ☐ Fourth

DISCUSSION TOPICS

1. These days, what products have high prices? _____

2. When was the last time you purchased something online? _____

3. What do you expect to do this weekend? _____

4. Do you know anybody who is extremely tall, fat, and/or smart? _____

5. Is it better to negotiate face-to-face or on the phone? Why? _____

6. If you were Jason, what would you do? _____

7. What is risky about purchasing scallops before they are harvested?

8. How would you try to sell this textbook?

_____
_____
_____
_____
_____
_____
_____
_____

Words to Know

Types (and brands) of Salmon in Japan *(see p. 44 for translation in Japanese)*

Chum salmon

- *tokishirazu* (prized for its rich oil content)

- *ginsei* (famous for its shiny color)

- mejika (famous for its soft, round body)

- *keiji* (20-30% fat throughout its body)

Pink salmon

Masu salmon

Chinook

Coho

Note...

Chum salmon are caught in 5 main areas in Hokkaido. The largest catch is in the Okhotsk Sea, followed by the Nemuro Straight, the East Pacific, the West Pacific and the Japan Sea. The catch sizes in these areas are similar, but the catch from the Japan Sea is the lowest (approx. 10% of the entire catch).

Juvenile chum live "in 139 streams held in 80 marine net pen sites before release" (Nagata, 2011). Chum salmon are caught using trap (set) net fishing methods.

Chum salmon is caught from late August to mid December. The Hokkaido chum salmon catch is the largest in the world.

READING - How to Negotiate in Japan

Many foreign companies find it difficult to negotiate with Japanese firms.

Because of the many cultural differences that exist when doing business with Japanese companies, foreigners have tried to better understand how Japanese culture can affect business dealings. The following list is an attempt to understand how Japanese culture influences negotiations.

1) **Emotional Sensitivity** (思いやり): Being careful, sensitive to the needs of others, and paying attention to details is important in Japan.

2) **Hiding Emotions** (感情を隠す): Japanese people show their feelings depending on who they are with. Hiding emotions is part of Japanese custom. The Japanese will normally not do business with someone they feel is arrogant or unpleasant.

3) **Showing Power**: Japanese people <u>don't like to show</u> their power. They <u>try to avoid</u> this kind of situation. They feel it is better to **conciliate** (機嫌を取る).

4) **Understanding "Amaeru"**: Japanese workers <u>expect</u> <u>to work</u> for the same company until they retire. They are very loyal to the company. The company's fate, they believe, is their fate.

5) **Group Spirit**: Decisions are made by groups, not individuals. This helps keep harmony in a company since 1 person can't be blamed for a bad decision.

6) **Delays Are Expected**: Because decisions are made by groups, the process can take longer than expected.

7) **Avoiding No**: Japanese people rarely say no. Instead, Japanese people might draw in a breath sharply, or say "It will be difficult to do". This will mean no. In Japan, it is common to tell people what they <u>want to</u> <u>hear</u>. Foreigners may believe a deal was made, but the opposite is true.

8) **The Value of Friendship**: The amount of time within a group helps decide the relationship. The longer the contact, the greater the value of the friendship. Trust takes time to develop, one step at a time.

9) **No Arguments, Please**: When a Japanese believes he is right, he will not argue. He will just stop talking.

READING COMPREHENSION

1. This article was written in 1970 by an American. Are his observations still true today? Explain your answer.

_____

2. Should decisions be made by a group or individual?

_____

3. What 3 things did you learn about foreigners from this article?

_____

4. Which of the 9 characteristics do you agree with the most, and why?

_____

5. Which of the 9 characteristics do you disagree with the most, and why?

_____

49

WRITING PRACTICE - Negotiation Quiz

Read the 7 situations below. After reading them, write what you would do in each situation.

1. You want to sell your house. You know you will be happy if you sell it for 20 000 000¥. A man knocks on your door. He offers (申し出る) you 22 000 000¥ in cash for your home. What do you do?

_____

_____

2. You want to buy a house. You find one you like. Its price is 20 000 000¥, but you only have 17 000 000¥. You meet the owner of the house, and tell him you are interested. You tell him you can only pay 17 000 000¥. He agrees to sell you the house for 17 000 000¥. What happened?

_____

_____

3. A young actor wants to become famous. He meets a movie director. The director says the actor would be perfect for a movie he is making. The director tells the actor that the pay will be very low. The actor is not famous yet, but if he does the movie, in the future he will be very rich. What should the actor do?

_____

_____

4. Your customer buys bread from you. One day, he tells you he will start making his own bread. The order will be the last. What should you do?

_____

_____

5. Your supplier calls to say your order will be delayed. The supply they have will be given to other customers. These customers pay a higher price and are considered long term priority customers. You protest. You just agreed to a price increase last week. What do you do?

_____

_____

6. You have started a new job. You will be getting married on March 14, and your soon-to-be wife wants a nice honeymoon: 1 week in Hawaii. On March 12, you ask your boss for a vacation. She is not happy, and asks, "How long?" What do you say?

_____

_____

7. You run a tour company. You are negotiating with a hotel in Spain. The hotel advertises a price 10 000¥ higher than the price now. What do you do?

_____

_____

GRAMMAR PRACTICE - Infinitives

These are verbs that act like nouns in a sentence. For example, in the sentence *I want to play tennis*

   WANT is the verb

   PLAY is the infinitive

The idea of PLAY. In this sentence, PLAY is a noun

Usually infinitives use **TO**

I had to go / I need to study / I like to travel

Here is a short list of infinitives. How many don't you know? _____

• Agree	• Expect	• Learn	• Prefer	• Wait
• Ask	• Fail	• Like	• Promise	• Want
• Can't stand	• Forget	• Love	• Refuse	• Wish
• Decide	• Hate	• Need	• Seem	• Would like
• Demand	• Hope	• Offer	• Start	
• Deserve	• Intend	• Plan	• Try	

PRACTICE

Answer the questions below using the correct Infinitive.

1. What do you hate to do on Sunday? _____

2. What do you hope to do next year? _____

3. When did you start to drink beer? _____

4. When did you decide to learn English? _____

5. What do you expect to receive for your birthday? _____

6. What do you sometimes forget to do? _____

7. Where would you like to live? _____

8. What do you wish you could do? _____

9. Which do you prefer to eat, sushi or salad? _____

10. What do you need to buy for your house? _____

Answer Key and Notes Unit 5

Vocabulary (p. 46)

1. extremely

2. expect

3. the price is too high

4. negotiate

5. fair price

6. just a moment

7. doesn't make sense

8. purchase

Listening Practice (p. 47)

1. Price

4. Good quality

7. Tsui

10. First

2. 360 ¥

5. 10% cheaper

8. Sizes and prices

3. No, I don't

6. Will lose money

9. Large

Salmon in Japan (p. 48)

漁獲地域、方法、時期

シロ鮭は、主に北海道の５つの地域で水揚げされています。最も漁獲量が多いのは、オホーツク海岸で、次に根室沖、太平洋側東海岸、そして、太平洋側西海岸です。水揚げ量は、どの地域でも同じくらいですが、日本海側が一番少なくなっております。（全体の１０％を占める）稚魚は、放流されるまでに、８０個の籠に入れられ、１３９カ所の小川で飼育されます。シロ鮭は、定置網で漁獲されています。８月の終わりから１２月の中旬までが漁獲時期です。

Negotiation Quiz (p. 50)

Here are some answers that would make you a strong negotiator.

1. Accept right away because he might find another house
2. Might have gotten a better price if you had offered a lower amount from the beginning
3. Actor knows he is good. If he sells himself cheap then he will get treated like that
4. Explain that costs may be higher doing it in-house, giving you the chance to discuss the reasons for this move
5. Ask what those customers pay and match the offer
6. Ask for 2 weeks and work your way down. Boss will respect your courage
7. Tell them you can not afford to pay that increase. Why should you pay that much per person?

Dialogue— Negotiation

Nori: May I speak to Mr. Tsui please.

(secretary): Just a moment, please.

Jason: Hello, Jason speaking.

Nori: Jason, how are you? It's Nori from Marusui. I read your email about the salmon and the king crab offer.

Jason: Your price is a little too high. I can get salmon here in Hong Kong at 360¥ a kilo, product of Canada, so it doesn't make sense for me to buy your salmon.

Nori: Our salmon prices might be high, but the quality is extremely good. The brand is mejika chum salmon, and only the best get that label.

Jason: Oh...Did you mention that in your email?

Nori: Yes, I did. And our king crab is about 10% cheaper than Hong Kong prices.

Jason: True. That price seems fair. But you are selling these products together. I'll take a loss on the salmon. I'm not interested in losing money.

Nori: We will be buying scallops soon, product of Hokkaido. We are purchasing a large amount. If you agree to this offer, I will contact you first for the scallops.

Jason: Send me the sizes and prices you expect for the scallops.

Unit 6 - Documents

● VOCABULARY

Finish

Yet

B/L

Invoice

Origin

Health certificate

Government agency

Chamber of Commerce

Attend

confirm

Finish the sentences with the correct word

1. A _____ is a document that lists products of a shipment.

2. Two hundred people will _____ his wedding.

3. Sometimes, a _____ can be slow.

4. To make sure food is safe, we need a _____.

5. The _____ is a business organization.

6. What time do you _____ work? Around 5pm.

7. I haven't eaten dinner _____. I'm so hungry.

8. I want to _____ if you can help me tomorrow or not.

LISTENING PRACTICE

In this dialogue, Nori san speaks with Sato san about preparing the salmon and king crab shipment. Listen to the dialogue between Sato san and Nori san. Listen to the dialogue once, and then answer the questions. After finishing the questions, check your answers. Listen to the dialogue a second time to check your answers one more time.

Questions for Dialogue 6: Documents

1. Has Nori finished his work?

☐ No, he didn't   ☐ No, he can't   ☐ No, he hasn't   ☐ No, he won't

2. Which document didn't Sato talk about?

☐ B/L   ☐ Packing List   ☐ Invoice   ☐ Origin

3. What document did Jason ask for?

☐ Health   ☐ King crab   ☐ Salmon   ☐ Hong Kong

4. Where will Nori get the document?

☐ Chamber of Commerce   ☐ He will make it   ☐ From Tokyo   ☐ From Sato san

5. The health certificate Jason wants is _____.

☐ Expensive   ☐ Fast   ☐ Long   ☐ Cheap

6. Where is Onishi?

☐ Brussels   ☐ Tokyo   ☐ Boston   ☐ Dubai

7. When will Onishi return?

☐ Today   ☐ Tomorrow   ☐ Next week   ☐ In 2 days

8. When will Sato and Nori meet the buyers?

☐ Morning   ☐ Afternoon   ☐ Night   ☐ Tomorrow

9. Where are the buyers from?

☐ Dubai   ☐ Brussels   ☐ America   ☐ Australia

10. What will Sato and Nori do with the buyers?

☐ Have dinner   ☐ Work   ☐ Watch a movie   ☐ Drink coffee

DISCUSSION TOPICS

1. What do you like about your job? _____

2. What don't you like about your job? _____

3. How many documents do you fill out every week? _____

4. Have you ever made a mistake at your job (i.e. documents)? _____

5. How long does it take you to complete an invoice? _____

6. Are all countries strict about documents? _____

7. Why would a country be strict about documents? _____

8. Hong Kong is famous for not being strict about documents. What do you think about this?

Words to Know

Health Certificates

When completing a Health Certificate, it is important to ask and know what customers need checked. Here is a list of common bacteria checked for in Health Certificates. Match the English words with their Japanese words.

1. DSP	A. リステリア菌
2. PSP	B. 黄色ブドウ球菌
3. V. cholera	C. 麻痺性貝中毒
4. Vibrio parahaemolyticus	D. クロロマイセチン
5. Escherichia coli	E. 腸炎ビブリオ
6. Staphylococcus aureus	F. コレラ菌
7. Listeria	G. クロラムフェニコール
8. Chloramphenicol	H. 大腸菌
9. Chloromycetin	I. 下痢性貝中毒

READING - What is HACCP?

The USA is the largest economy in the world. If a company wants to export seafood to the US market, the products need to be processed using HACCP guidelines to ensure their safety. But what is HACCP?

HACCP stands for Hazard Analysis and Critical Control Points.

Ummm...what does that mean?

Well, it is a system to make sure food is safe. It was started in the 1960s for NASA. It was used for astronauts. Just imagine if people in space got sick because they ate bad food. It would be a disaster.

That's true, but how does it work?

It works by processing food safely. HACCP is a system that checks each step used to prepare food. By following HACCP, food can be tested in stages instead of only testing food after production.

Sounds complicated. How many parts does HACCP have?

HACCP has 2 parts. The first part is to make a list of things that can cause the food to be unsafe—we call this hazard analysis. Part two is deciding the best place to control the hazards during production—we call this the critical control point for that hazard.

That's hard to understand. Can you give an example?

Okay. When seafood is processed, every step is checked for hazards. This includes raw seafood, ingredients added to the seafood, handling, storage, and distribution. If there is a toxin or chemical in the seafood, HACCP helps find when and where this happens and tries to stop or control it. This is part 2 of HACCP, the critical control point.

I don't understand.

HACCP helps find and fix problems. Which part of this story can cause a health problem: You bought some shrimps at a seafood market, brought them home in ice, put them in the fridge, and ate them 6 days later.

Eating them 6 days later. That's a bit too long.

Exactly. Fresh shrimp should be eaten within 2-3 days. Six days is the problem, and that is what HACCP does, it finds ways to keep food safe and fresh to eat.

READING COMPREHENSION

1. Why is HACCP important to exporters?

_____

2. What does HACCP check for?

_____

3. How many parts does HACCP have?

_____

4. When is it not safe to eat shrimps kept in a fridge?

_____

WRITING PRACTICE - An Invoice

An invoice is a bill given to a buyer. On an invoice, there is important information about cost of products, quantity of products, and method of payment. Look at the invoice below, and fill in the missing information. Listen to the dialogue and take notes while listening.

Marusui Sapporo Chuo Suisan Co. LTD.

Kita 12-jo, Nishi 20-chome, No. 2-1 Chuo Ku

Sapporo, Japan

[Buying Company's Address is here]

AWB No.: AB2009-589X

Final Destination: (2) _____

Vessel/Voy. No.: TG671

ETD: 02/24/2015

ETA: (3) _____

[Date]

INVOICE

Invoice No.: Botan0001

Invoice date: (1) _____

No.	Description	Quantity (ctn)	Net Weight	Unit Price	Amount	Country Of Origin
1.	Fresh Uni	5	50 kg	(7) _____	175 000 yen	Japan
2.	Fresh Hotate	(5) _____	(6) _____	3300/kg	165 000 yen	Japan
3.	(4) _____	2	50kg	2700/kg	(8) _____	Japan

Country of Origin: Japan

Net Weight: 150kg

Gross Weight: (9) _____

Total Packings: 12

Bank Ref: (10) _____

Bank Address: Kita 12-jo, Nishi 14-chome,

No. 5, Chuo-Ku, Sapporo, Japan

Marusui Sapporo Chuo Suisan

GRAMMAR PRACTICE - Understanding Sentences

Circle the best answer for each question.

The sentences below demonstrate different ways we use adjectives and adverbs.
Basically, adjectives describe nouns, for example, a TALL man or a YELLOW ball. Tall and yellow are 2 kinds of adjectives.
Adverbs describe verbs or actions. Adverbs that end in *ly*, for example, SLOWLY or QUIETLY, usually go after a verb.

1. He talks *slow / slowly*, so it is *easy / easily* to understand him.

2. These flowers smell *nice / nicely*.

3. Please look *close / closely* at the painting on the wall.

4. He is never *late / lately* for this class.

5. This chair is very *comfortable / comfortably*.

6. He runs quite *fast / fastly*.

7. Mark looked very *happy / happily* in his new suit.

8. Please close the door *quiet / quietly*.

9. Please give more homework to Hana and **me / I**.

10. The cat and dog are playing with **another / each other / the other**.

11. My friend and **I / me / my** like to play poker.

12. Is the coat hanging on the door **you / your / yours?**

13. **Nobody / Anybody / Somebody** in our class is from Africa.

14. The person **that / who / which** likes pineapples is Toma.

15. My mother-in-law enjoys taking trips by **sheself / herself / myself.**

Answer Key and Notes Unit 6

Vocabulary (p. 54)

1) B/L or invoice   2) attend   3) government agency   4) health certificate

5) Chamber of Commerce   6) finish   7) yet   8) confirm

Listening (p. 55)

1) No, he hasn't   2) packing list   3) health   4) Chamber of Commerce   5) cheap

6) Dubai   7) tomorrow   8) night   9) America   10) have dinner

Discussion (p. 56)

1) I   2) C   3) F   4) E   5) H

6) B   7) A   8) G   9) D

Reading (p. 57)

1. Exporters need to have HACCP certified products to sell in the US market.
2. HACCP is a system for checking food safety.
3. Things such as toxins and harmful chemicals.
4. Two.
5. After 2 or 3 days.

Writing (p. 58)

1) February 15   2) Bangkok   3) February 24, 2015   4) kegani (or hair crab)   5) 5

6) 50   7) 3,500 yen   8) 135 000 yen   9) 210kg   10) Hokkaido Bank

Grammar Practice (p. 59)

1) slowly / is   2) nice   3) closely   4) late   5) comfortable   6) fast   7) happy

8) quietly   9) me   10) each other   11) I   12) yours   13) Nobody   14) who   15) herself

Dialogue Unit 6—Documents

Sato san: Nori, have you finished everything?
Nori: Ummm...

Sato: Have you finished all the documents yet?
Nori: I'm almost...yes, I'm almost...

Sato: You just need the B/L, origin, and invoice, right?
Nori: Jason contacted me yesterday, and he also asked for a health certificate.

Sato: Does he need one from the government agency, or the chamber of commerce.
Nori: He asked for the one from the chamber of commerce. It's cheap.

Sato: Why don't you ask Onishi to contact the Sapporo Chamber of Commerce for you?

Nori: I can't. He is attending a trade show in Dubai. He'll get back tomorrow.

Sato: Then finish the documents, confirm the shipment and date with Mr. Nikaido at Hokkai Transportation, and get ready for tonight.

Nori: Tonight?

Sato: Yes. We are going out for dinner with some buyers from America.

Writing Practice (p. 51) — Dialogue

Onishi—Nori, can you help me with something?

Nori – Sure. What's the problem?

O—I need to send this invoice today, but could you just check it first?

N—Let me see it? Okay, the invoice is for today, February 15, going to Bangkok on flight TG 671. What airline is TG?

O—Thai Air. There is a flight once a day to Bangkok from Chitose in the morning.

N—I see. So the arrival date is the same as the departure date, right?

O—Yes, February 24. And we are shipping 3 products: fresh uni, kegani, and hotate.

N—I would write the English names for those products. It's sea urchin, hair crab, and scallops. Okay, and the amount of sea urchin and scallops are the same, and 2 cartons of hair crab. The weight of the sea urchin and scallops are the same, right?

O—That's right.

N—Okay, good...uni is expensive, 200 yen more per kilogram than scallops...okay, and the gross weight is 210kg. Looks good.

O—Can you sign it then? Next to the Hokkaido Bank information.

Unit 7 - Inspection

⬤ VOCABULARY

Sanitary conditions

Bacteria

Determine

Expectations

Expired

Best before date

Running water

Drain

Estimate

Glazing

Inspected

Brine

Finish the sentences with the correct word

1. Don't eat that meat. It _____ last week.

2. My _____ is blocked with hair. YUCK!

3. _____ is very salty, so you shouldn't drink it.

4. The _____ at this factory are excellent. It has HACCP.

5. After they _____ the box, they found some _____, so nobody could eat the food inside.

6. Scallops have about 10% _____ to keep them fresh.

7. I _____ it will cost much money to buy the BMW.

LISTENING PRACTICE

Nori successfully sold the salmon and king crab to Jason, the Hong Kong buyer. After finishing the questions, check your answers. Listen to the dialogue a second time to check your answers one more time.

Questions for Dialogue 7: Interested in Scallops

1. Why was Sato san happy?

   ☐ The weather   ☐ The shipment   ☐ The holidays   ☐ The documents

2. What is Jason interested in buying?

   ☐ Scallops   ☐ Sea urchin   ☐ Salmon   ☐ King crab

3. Why might it be difficult to sell the product to Jason?

   ☐ The demand   ☐ The cost   ☐ The supply   ☐ Nori

4. Is demand for scallops low this year?

   ☐ Yes, they are   ☐ Yes, it is   ☐ No, they aren't   ☐ No, it isn't

5. What don't Hong Kong buyers usually need?

   ☐ B/L   ☐ Health certificate   ☐ Country of Origin   ☐ Insurance

6. How much is the certificate?

   ☐ 12 000   ☐ 12 500   ☐ 13 000   ☐ 13 500

7. Who has to pay for the certificate?

   ☐ Government   ☐ Nori   ☐ Sato   ☐ Jason

8. What does Nori have to find out for the inspection?

   ☐ Price of scallops   ☐ Price of certificate   ☐ Type of bacteria   ☐ Shipping date

9. Can the government agency be slow?

   ☐ Yes, they can   ☐ Yes, they do   ☐ Yes, it can   ☐ Yes, it does

10. How long might it take to get the certificate?

   ☐ 1 day   ☐ 1 week   ☐ 2 days   ☐ 2 weeks

DISCUSSION TOPICS

1. What foreign products do you like to buy? _____

2. If someone inspected your home, which room would be dirtiest? _____

3. What do you think about foreign food? _____

4. Have you ever had food poisoning? _____

5. Besides Japan, which country's food do you trust? _____

6. What kinds of food don't you usually eat? _____

7. How do you prepare for this class? _____

8. Do you need a reservation at your favorite restaurant?

_____

_____

_____

_____

*Useful Information...*Scallop Sizes:

When exporting to the US, buyers often ask for sizes and quantities in pounds (lb). Here is a conversion list. These are approximate quantities, so inspecting products before shipping is important

Scallop Sizes in kg	Scallop Sizes in pounds
3L (10-15/kg)	5 - 7 per pound
2L (16-20/kg)	7 - 9/lb
L (21-25/kg)	9 – 11/lb
M (26-30/kg)	12 – 14/lb
S (31-35/kg)	14 – 16/lb
2S (36-40/kg)	16 – 18/lb
3S (41-45/kg)	18 – 20/lb
4S (46-50/kg)	21 – 23/lb

READING - Inspection Process, Scallops & King Crab

Inspecting products does not only mean checking if the product is in sanitary condition and free from bacteria. A lot of information is gathered for a product inspection. This information helps buyers determine whether the products they are buying meet with their expectations.

The story below explains two types of inspections done at a seafood trading company in Sapporo, Japan. Customers can ask for many things to be examined and inspected, so these examples are not the rule.

I have done 2 kinds of inspections for customers. The first inspection was done on scallops. First I wrote down the company name, and dates of production and expiration.

Next, we opened the 10kg carton, and inspected each box inside. We opened one of the boxes (1kg) of L-sized scallops, and weighed the scallops (1075g + 10g for bag). After opening the bag of scallops and placing them in a bowl, we weighed the box (95g) and the vinyl bag (10g).

All of this information went into an inspection report for buyers. Next, we counted the number of frozen scallops (22), and weighed each one. After this, we defrosted the scallops in running water for approximately 15 minutes, weighing them again.

Next, we let them sit and drain for 1 hour, weighing them once again. In total, we had 3 measurements for the scallops: Frozen, 15 minutes defrosted, 1 hour defrosted.

We looked for color, took photos of the box, label, and the bag of scallops. We also estimated the amount of glazing used for the scallops. A proper inspection reduces the chance of unhappy customers.

We also inspected a shipment of king crabs. We inspected this product by measuring boxes (L/W/H), taking 3 photos of each box (box, label, product inside), weighing for gross weight, and writing down catch and expiry dates.

When inspecting the king crab, we cracked a leg to test for space between shell and meat. The less space the better. More space means more brine gets between the parts, making for a salty product. This should be noted in an inspection report. We tasted the king crab, and decided it was not salty but sweet and delicious.

It was also my dinner that night.

READING COMPREHENSION

1. What kind of information is gathered in an inspection?

_____

2. Why do you think the inspectors measured the scallops 3 times?

_____

3. What do you think glazing means?

_____

4. What do inspectors look for in king crabs?

_____

5. Why do you think the inspectors measured the box size?

_____

WRITING PRACTICE - Inspection Email

Using the information in the charts, write an email to a buyer interested in purchasing an order of mentaiko. This is an email to a future customer, so be sure to use the right ton

Country of Origin	Pieces/crtn	Average Weight	Expiry Date	Best Before Date
Korea	2-3	203g/piece	Aug., 2016	Apr., 2016

Processing Date	Price		Quantity Available
February 10, 2015	Cold Storage Fukuoka: 530 yen/kg		10t

From:

To:

Cc:

Sent:

Subject:

GRAMMAR PRACTICE - Verb Tenses

Time is important in life. We save time, make time, do things from time to time, take time outs, time off and work over-time if we don't get to work on time. It is also very important for verb tenses. Time controls which verb tenses to use in a sentence. Read the following sentences, and use the correct verb tense to finish the sentence.

EXAMPLE: In 2 days , I _____ visit Dalian, China. (answer: **will** or **am going to visit**)

1. I _____ (**live**) in Japan for 4 years, and I still live in Japan`.

2. Two days ago, he _____ (**study**) hard for a test.

3. These days, she _____ (**try**) to eat more salmon.

4. Since 9am, we _____ (**work**) on these documents (still working).

5. Recently, I _____ (**meet**) many customers.

6. Last night at 11pm, I _____ (**read**) these documents.

7. Tonight at 11pm, I _____ (**take**) a flight to Taiwan.

8. As soon as I wake up tomorrow, I _____ (**call**) you.

9. Whenever I _____ (**drink**) too much sake, I get tired.

10. While he _____ (**come**) here, he met his old friend.

11. The first time I _____ (**visit**) the USA, it _____ (**be**) a business trip.

12. They _____ (**go**) to the airport at 5pm.

13. The other day, she _____ (**buy**) one container of botan shrimp.

14. The day before yesterday, he _____ (**find**) his book.

15. The day after tomorrow, she _____ (**quit**) her job (100%).

Answer Key and Notes Unit 7

Vocabulary (p. 62)

1) don't usually   2) reservation   3) guess   4) interested in   5) be prepared
6) good job   7) seem   8) demand

Listening (p. 63)

1) the shipment   2) scallops   3) the demand   4) No, it isn't   5) Health Certificate
6) 120 000   7) Jason   8) type of bacteria   9) Yes, it can   10) 2 weeks

Reading (p. 65)

1. An inspection can collect data such as weight, product sizes, dates, photos, etc.
2. To check how much water the scallops contain.
3. Glazing is the amount of ice covering the product to safely ship it.
4. Inspectors measure the space between the meat and the shell.
5. When shipping, we need to meausre the box sizes to know how much space they take in a container.

Writing (p. 66)

Dear Kessarin,

Thank you for your email. Regarding the mentaiko, this product was caught and processed in Korea. It was processed on February 10, 2015, and has an expiry date of August, 2016. We are offering this product in sets of 2 boxes. Each box contains 2-3 pieces of mentaiko (4-6 pieces per set).

The average   weight per piece is 203g. The price for this product is 530 yen/kg. This is the cold-storage price (Fukuoka), and does not include document or shipping fees.

If interested, please let me know. We have approx. 10t available.

Best regards,

Nori

Grammar Practice (p. 67)

1) have lived   2) studied   3) is trying   4) have been working   5) am meeting   6) was reading OR read   7) am going to take   8) will call   9) drink   10) was coming   11) visited / was
12) will OR am going to go   13) bought   14) found   15) is going to quit

Dialogue - Interested in Scallops

Sato: Good job on the shipment to Hong Kong.
Nori: Thank you Sato san. Now Jason is interested in the scallops we have. But he says the price is a little high.

S: Of course he says that. Did you tell him that these scallops have HACCP?
N: Yes, and I also told him that demand is high this year. Also, he wants a health certificate.

S: Hong Kong buyers don't usually ask for that.
N: I guess he might have an American buyer he is selling to.

S: How much is the health certificate?

N: About 12 000 yen, which he has to pay for, so the price seems high.

S: Find out what he needs inspected...the type of bacteria...and contact the government agency to make a reservation. This can take a long time if they are busy. It is better to be prepared.

N: I already did that. They said it would take about 2 weeks to complete.

S: They are really slow these days. I wonder if there is another way to get this product inspected...

Unit 8 Payment

VOCABULARY

About the _____

Offered

To be honest

Willing to pay

I'll get back to you

We can work with that number

Accept

Loading

Details

I'll get right on it

Bye for now

Finish the sentences with the correct word

1. What are you talking about? Please give me more _____?

2. Boss: I need the report by tomorrow. It's very important

   Worker: Okay boss, _____.

3. She _____ me a new job, but I said no. I like my job now.

4. I am only _____ 700yen/kg for that. That's my best price.

5. I'll see you when you come back from Hawaii. _____.

6. Hi Lee, long time no see. I read your email, and I want to ask you
   _____ lobsters. Where are they from?

7. _____, I usually buy from your competitor, but these days, I am
   not happy with his service.

8. Your price is too high. I can't _____ your offer. Please give me a better price.

LISTENING PRACTICE

In this dialogue, Jason wants to buy scallops, and Nori answers some questions about payment methods. Listen to the dialogue once, and then answer the questions. After finishing the questions, check your answers. Listen to the dialogue a second time to check your answers one more time.

Questions for Dialogue 8: Payment Method

1. What is Nori calling Jason about?

   ☐ About shipping   ☐ About salmon   ☐ About surf clam   ☐ About scallops

2. Does another buyer want to buy the scallops?

   ☐ Yes   ☐ No

3. Is the price FOB, CIF, C&F, or something else?

   ☐ FOB   ☐ CIF   ☐ C&F   ☐ Something else

4. How much are the 3S scallops?

   ☐ 2800 yen/kg   ☐ 2900 yen/kg   ☐ 3000 yen/kg   ☐ 3100 yen/kg

5. How much are the M scallops?

   ☐ 2800 yen/kg   ☐ 2900 yen/kg   ☐ 3000 yen/kg   ☐ 3100 yen/kg

6. When does Jason call back Nori?

   ☐ After 10 minutes   ☐ After 20 minutes   ☐ After 1 hour   ☐ After 2 hours

7. Does Nori's company accept LC?

   ☐ No, it can't   ☐ No, it don't   ☐ No, he won't   ☐ No, it doesn't

8. Why not?

   ☐ Small company   ☐ New customer   ☐ Bad banks   ☐ Large amount

9. Nori's company must get payment before_____.

   ☐ Loading   ☐ Shipping   ☐ Saturday   ☐ Eating

10. Which one DOESN'T Jason want Nori to send him by email?

   ☐ Details   ☐ Health Certificate   ☐ Invoice   ☐ Photos

DISCUSSION TOPICS

1. How do you pay for food at a restaurant?   Cash / Credit Card / Bank Card / other

_____

2. How many credit cards do you have?

_____

3. How often do you use a credit card?

_____

4. Why do companies prefer cash payments?

_____

5. Should companies use LC payments (Letter of Credit)?

_____

6. If you lend money to someone, when do you expect the person to give back the money?

_____

7. Do you think lending money to friends is okay? Why or why not?

_____

8. What is the difference between FOB Japan and C&F Hong Kong?

_____

Shipping & Payment Terms to Know

For business acronyms (略語) explained in Japanese, go to www.boueki.caplan.jp/vocabulary.html#07

FOB: Free On Board, the exporting company pays for all costs until the goods are loaded for shipment.

TT: Telegraphic Transfer, It is the transfer of funds ,from the buyer's bank to selling company's bank

CIF: Cost, Insurance and Freight; A trading term requiring the seller to arrange for the transportation of goods by sea to a port of destination, and provide the buyer with the documents necessary to obtain the goods from the transport company.

C&F: Cost and Freight, the same as CIF (Cost/Freight/Insurance) except the shipment price does not include insurance. The price does include all shipment expenses up to a determined port of destination.

LC: Letter Of Credit, a document issued to provide a payment undertaking within a certain amount of time after the buyer receives the shipment.

READING - Japanese Prefer Cash to Checks, Cards

My daughter's school called and reminded me that we had to pay 400,000¥ for tuition. I asked how to pay. ``Just bring the cash over some night on the way home from work.`` Just bring the cash? Carrying cash to pay a big bill seemed strange. To the Japanese, however, writing a check to the school -- was simply unthinkable.

Although Japan has the world's largest banks, a personal checking account is not common in Japan. Some Japanese never write a check their whole lives.

There are no paychecks; in fact, it is illegal to pay salaries by check. Most people have their pay wired to the bank. However, tens of millions of people get paid with an envelope filled with cash.

Many businesses, particularly companies that work overseas, have checking accounts. But this is not true for regular people.` Almost no people or families have checking accounts.

There are many theories as to why Japanese people do not use checks.

Some say the reason is cultural: ``It has to do with the concept of *haji*, or personal shame,`` said Kiyoshi Murakami, of J.P. Morgan.``Traditionally, people felt shame if they did not pay a bill immediately, in cash.``

Some people say checks are not popular because Japanese people are not used to signing their names. The normal way to authorize financial or other documents is with a personal seal, or *hanko*, with the Chinese characters of a person's family name.

Another possible reason is that people don't need checks in this peaceful country. There is no word in Japanese for mugging.

Money transfers between banks are common, and are used for regular payments like mortgages, car payments, and rice delivery. Credit cards are still not as popular as cash in Japan.

Sometimes, only cash can be used. People invited to a wedding, a graduation party or a funeral should give a cash gift -- from $35 to $3,500 -- to the host. In North America, wedding guests often give a check for a gift.

READING COMPREHENSION

1. Why do you think Japanese people and businesses prefer cash transactions?

2. Have things changed in Japan since 1991 regarding cash, credit cards, or other forms of payments?

3. What is different between Japanese and American families?

4. Do you ever forget to pay your bills on time? If yes, what happened?

5. How often do you write a check?

WRITING PRACTICE - Read the information, and complete the invoice

The Bill of Lading is GR452. The ETD is the same as the invoice date. It takes 3 days from Japan to Thailand. The gross weight is 50kg more than the net weight. All products are from Japan except 1. The remarks refer to the freight charges. The ship's number is Z6557PLY. And cartons are a kind of packing.

01/14/2014

Marusui Sapporo Chuosuisan Co., LTD

kita 12-jo-Nishi 20-Chome No.2-1 Chuo-KU
Sapporo, Japan TEL (81)-11-643-1234

TO:
Oishi FOODS (THAILAND) CO., LTD
140, 1-2A FL., Surhat Bldg., Soi Tangloplaza,
Surawong RD., Suriyawong, Bangrak, Bangkok, 10500, Thailand
TEL: (66) 2-513-7010

Commercial Invoice

Invoice No.: OF0001

Invoice Date: Jan. 14, 2014

B/L No.: _____

Final Destination: _____

Vessel/Voy. No.: _____

ETD (city, country, date of dep.): _____

ETA (city, country, date of arr.): _____

No.	Description	Quantity (ctn)	Net Weight (kg)	Unit Price (kg)	Amount	Country of Origin
1.	Frozen Mackerel	100	1000	¥_____	¥974,000	Russia
2.	Frozen Hokki	56	560	¥ 1,299	¥727,440	Japan
3.	Frozen Scallops	74	740	¥ 2,850	¥_____	Japan
4.	Frozen Salmon	97	970	¥ 800	¥776,000	_____

Country of origin: _____

Net Weight: _____

Gross Weight: _____

Total Packings: _____

REMARKS:

    Documents, L/C, etc: ¥35,000

    Export expenses, etc.: ¥155,000

Sub-Total (FOB Value): ¥4,586,440

Freight Charges: _____

C&F Bangkok, Thailand **GRAND TOTAL** : ¥4,776,440

* Invoice must also include the exporter/selling company's **bank information**. See p. 50 for an example.

GRAMMAR PRACTICE - Present Tense

In the photos below, write one sentence describing what the person or people are doing.

In pictures, the verb tense is always in the present tense (現在形).

You can write more than one sentence.

1.

_____

_____

_____

2.

_____

_____

_____

3.

_____

_____

_____

4.

_____

_____

_____

5.

_____

_____

_____

6.

_____

_____

_____

7.

_____

_____

_____

8.

_____

_____

_____

9.

_____

_____

_____

10.

_____

_____

_____

Answer Key and Notes Unit 8

Vocabulary (p. 70)

1) details   2) I'll get right on it   3) offered   4) willing to pay   5) Bye for now
6) about the   7) To be honest   8) accept

Listening (p. 71)

1) scallops   2) Yes   3) C&F Hong Kong   4) 2,800/kg   5) 3,100/kg
2) 20 minutes later   7) No, it doesn't   8) new customer   9) loading
10) Health Certificate

Reading (p. 73) - *There are many possible answers to all of these questions*

1. It is easier for the people who receive the payment in cash.
2. A little. People use credit cards more these days.
3. Paying school tuition or giving a check for a wedding gift.
4. (Open Answer)
5. I write a check _____ time(s) a year.   OR   I never write a check.

Writing (p. 74)

1) GR452   2) Bangkok   3) X6557PLY   4) Sapporo, Hokkaido 01/14/2014   5) Bangkok, Thailand

01/17/2014   6) ¥974/kg   7) ¥727,440   8) Japan   9) Japan & Russia

10) 3,270kg   11) 3,320kg   12) 327   13) ¥190,000

Grammar (p. 75)

1. He is swimming.
2. He is picking up a box (or lifting a box).
3. He is giving the man money.
4. He is sleeping
5. She is cooking.
6. He is taking a picture.
7. They are celebrating (or drinking).
8. He is delivering a package.
9. He is fishing.
10. They are bowing (or greeting).

Listening Dialogue

Nori (on the phone): May I speak to Jason, please?
Jason (on the phone): This is Jason. How can I help you?

N: Jason, hi it's Nori from Japan. How are you?
J: Nori, hi. Thanks for calling. I'm fine, and you?

N: Very good thank you. About the scallops, the best price I can offer you is 2800/kg for the 3S and 3100 for the M scallops. To be honest, I have another buyer willing to pay that price, if you aren't interested.
J: This price is FOB Japan or C&F Hong Kong?

N: C&F Hong Kong.

J: Nori, let me check a few things first. I'll get back to you in an hour.

N: Okay Jason, talk to you soon

———————— 20 minutes later ————————

J: Hello Nori. Thanks for waiting. Okay, we can work with those numbers. Does your company use LC?

N: Sorry, not with new customers. We only accept cash patments or TT payments before loading.

J: I see. Alright, please email me with the details, photos of the products, and an invoice.

N: I'll get right on it. Thank you very much.

J: No, thank you. Okay, bye for now.

Unit 9 Shipping Company

⬤ VOCABULARY

Match the words on the left to the meanings on the right

1) A shipment of

2) A container

3) Length

4) Width

5) Height

6) Cartons

7) Sent

8) I'll get back to you

a) 長さ

b) カートン

c) 〜の出荷

d) 折り返しご連絡致します

e) 送信しました

f) 幅

g) コンテナ

h) 高さ

LISTENING PRACTICE

In this dialogue, Nori speaks with Yosuke from the Nissui Transportation Company about a container for frozen scallops. Listen to the dialogue once, and then answer the questions. After finishing the questions, check your answers. Listen to the dialogue a second time to check your answers one more time.

Questions for Dialogue 9: Shipping Companies

1. What is the name of Yosuke's company?

   ☐ Hokkai   ☐ Mumbai   ☐ Nissui   ☐ Tempui

2. What does Nori want to send to Hong Kong?

   ☐ His girlfriend   ☐ Sato san   ☐ Salmon   ☐ Scallops

3. What is the size of the container?

   ☐ 20f   ☐ 30f   ☐ 40f   ☐ 50f

4. When will Yosuke get back to Nori?

   ☐ In the morning   ☐ In the afternoon   ☐ In the evening   ☐ February 11

5. How many cartons does Nori want to ship?

   ☐ 500   ☐ 700   ☐ 900   ☐ scallops

6. When does Nori want to send the shipment of scallops?

   ☐ In about 3 weeks   ☐ In about 3 days   ☐ In the afternoon   ☐ To Hong Kong

7. What do you think HEIGHT means?

   ☐ How much   ☐ How tall   ☐ How long   ☐ How heavy

8. Does Nori want to ship the scallops FOB or C&F?

   ☐ FOB   ☐ C&F

9. What does the word QUOTE mean?

   ☐ Container size   ☐ Number of boxes   ☐ Time of shipment   ☐ Price

10. What is wrong with Yosuke?

   ☐ Too tired   ☐ Too busy   ☐ Too much sake   ☐ Caught a cold

DISCUSSION TOPICS

1. Do you think the price of shipping is expensive (i.e. letters, packages, containers...)?

_____

2. If you had the chance, would you sail across the Pacific Ocean on a cargo ship?

_____

3. What do you think about Japan Post (slow, expensive, efficient, professional...)?

_____

4. What is the width of your stomach?

_____

5. Did you ever have any bad experiences shipping something?

_____

6. Is price the most important reason to select a shipping company?

_____

7. How important are logistics for a trading company?

_____

8. What kinds of charges do shipping companies put on invoices?

_____

USEFUL INFORMATION - Carton Sizes and Containers

In the dialogue, Yosuke asks Nori about the length, width, and height of the cartons. Yosuke needs to know this information. He has to know the EXACT size of the cartons so he can calculate the space the cartons will need. If the cartons are not placed properly, they can fall and break during the trip.

CALCULATING VOLUME

To find the volume of a shipment, we multiply (x) **length x width x height ÷ 1 000 000 x # of cartons.**

EXAMPLE: 48 (length) x 41 (width) x 26 (height) = 51, 168

51,168 ÷ 1,000,000 = .051168

.051168 x 500 (cartons) = **25.584m³**

A 20 ft reefer container can deliver a shipment size of approximately 28.2m³ .

READING - History of Shipping in Japan

Japan is an **archipelago** (列島). It has 1000s of islands, and from the tip of Hokkaido to southern Okinawa, Japan is about 3000km long. To Japanese people, the sea is very important. Japanese art, diet, history, and identity have been influenced by the sea from the beginning.

During the Edo Period (1603—1868), contact and trade with foreigners was **limited** (制限されていた). In the 1700s and 1800s, about 1-2 ships every year arrived in Japan. Japanese fishermen didn't fish far from Japanese shores. Their boats could not travel far. But this changed in 1853.

Admiral Matthew Perry arrived with his 'Black Ships' on July 8, 1853. He **forced** (強制した) Japan to open up its ports to foreign traders. Soon after this, the Meiji Restoration began in Japan. From 1868 to 1912, many changes happened in Japan. In a short time, Japan became a modernized nation because it started to look for information in other countries.

The Japanese Navy quickly modernized. It became strong and powerful, and Japanese shipping companies did the same. Companies like Mitsubishi began trading across the Pacific and **throughout** (全域) Asia. Mitsubishi Mail Steamship Company started a service to China. It was the first Japanese company to open an overseas shipping route. One of the products Japan traded was seafood, and seafood helped Japan become a modern country.

By the 1920s, Japanese companies were catching **large amounts of** (大量の) seafood. Processing companies were canning salmon, tuna, shrimp, and whale for export. Some people call this "Japan's Ocean Empire". Fishermen were traveling the world, selling seafood in Japan and to foreign buyers.

Selling seafood **abroad** (海外で) helped Japan get **foreign currencies** (外貨). With this money, Japan bought oil, iron, and rubber. By the 1930s, Japan's fishing fleet was the largest in the world. Shipping companies like Mitsubishi brought products like oil, iron, and rubber to Japan, and this made Japan a strong, modern nation.

READING COMPREHENSION

1. How do you think the sea influences (影響をもたらした) Japan?

_____

2. What do you think about the American, Adm. Perry?

_____

3. Which country do you think influenced Japan the most?

_____

4. How often do you eat canned food?

_____

5. What do you think made Japan a strong, modern country?

_____

GRAMMAR PRACTICE - Past Tense

In the reading section, Shipping in Japan, we can read many <u>verbs</u> used in the past tense. Here is a list of the past tense verbs found in the reading. Match the meaning of the English verb with the Japanese verb.

1) Arrived	4) Bought	7) Did	10) Helped	13) Modernized	16) Were canning
2) Became	5) Brought	8) Forced	11) Influenced	14) Started	17) Were catching
3) Began	6) Changed	9) Happened	12) Made	15) Traded	18) Were traveling

a) 近代化	f) 起こった	k) 缶詰していた	p) 開始した
b) ～した	g) 助けた	l) 始まった	q) 影響を受けた
c) 強制的した	h) 水揚げされていた	m) 変更した	r) もたらした
d) となった	i) 作った	n) 海外取引した	
e) 旅行していた	j) 着いた	o) 購入した	

1) _____ 4) _____ 7) _____ 10) _____ 13) _____ 16) _____

2) _____ 5) _____ 8) _____ 11) _____ 14) _____ 17) _____

3) _____ 6) _____ 9) _____ 12) _____ 15) _____ 18) _____

Here is a list of the 40 most common irregular English verbs. How many of them do you know? _____

1. Say	2. Make	3. Go	4. Take	5. Come	6. See	7. Know
8. Get	9. Give	10. Find	11. Think	12. Tell	13. Become	14. Show
15. Leave	16. Feel	17. Put	18. Bring	19. Begin	20. Hold	21. Keep
22. Write	23. Stand	24. Hear	25. Let	26. Mean	27. Set	28. Meet
29. Run	30. Pay	31. Sit	32. Speak	33. Lie	34. Send	35. Read
36. Grow	37. Lose	38. Break	39. Choose	40. Understand		

Sentence Practice: Make a sentence with each of the verbs below.

1. Make: _____

2. Put: _____

3. Send: _____

4. Show: _____

5. Break: _____

6. Speak: _____

WRITING PRACTICE

Part I - Answer each question using a full sentence.

1. What time did you come here today? _____

2. What did you make for dinner yesterday? _____

3. Who did you send an email to last week? _____

4. Last month, who did you meet? _____

5. What did you bring here today? _____

6. What were you doing last night at 10pm? _____

7. Two days ago, what did you buy? _____

8. When you were young, what did your parents force you to do?

_____

9. Yesterday, what did you read? _____

10. Where did you go last year? _____

Part II - Use the correct verb to finish the sentence. Use the list of verbs below, and try to use each verb only 1 time.

> Arrived, became, began, bought, brought, changed, did, forced, happened, helped, influenced, modernized, traded

1. What _____ to you? I thought we had a promise to meet at 2pm?

2. It _____ to rain, so we cancelled the baseball game.

3. In the past, Europeans _____ gold for spices.

4. What _____ you do last night?

5. Our company _____ its computers and many workers like their new computers.

6. The man _____ some flowers for his girlfriend.

7. I _____ here at 6am, but our meeting was at 7am. I was too early.

8. The kind lady _____ the little boy tie his shoelaces.

9. The price of shrimps _____ very expensive after the powerful storm.

10. Our boss _____ us to a nice restaurant yesterday, and he paid for dinner.

Answer Key and Notes Unit 9

Vocabulary (p.78)

A) length   B) cartons   C) shipment of   D) I'll get back to you
E) send   F) width   G) container   H) height

Listening (p. 79)

1. Nissui   2. scallops   3. 20f   4. In the afternoon   5. 500
6. In about 3 weeks   7. How tall   8. C&F   9. price   10. Caught a cold

Grammar Practice (p. 82)

A) 13   B) 7   C) 8   D) 2   E) 18   F) 9   G) 10   H) 17   I) 1   J) 12   K) 16   L) 3
M) 6   N) 15   O) 4   P) 14   Q) 11   R) 5

Writing Practice (p. 83)

1) happened   2) began   3) traded   4) did   5) modernized
6) bought   7) arrived   8) helped   9) became   10) brought

Dialogue - Shipping Companies

Yosuke (rep for Nissui Transportation): Nissui Transportation. Yosuke speaking. How can I help you?
Nori: hello Yosuke. It's Nori. How are you?

Y: I'm fine, Nori, but I caught a cold. What can I do for you today?
N: I'm sending a shipment of frozen scallops to Hong Kong. Can you give me a price for this shipment. I need a 20f reefer container.

Y: Okay. What size are the boxes and how many boxes do you have?
N: The boxes are 48cm length, 41cm width and 26cm height. And there are 500 cartons.

Y: Got it. FOB or C&F?
N: C&F Hong Kong.

Y: When do you want to send the shipment?
N: In about 3 weeks...so I want the shipment sent on February 11.

Y: Okay, I'll get back to you this afternoon with a quote...Anything else?
N: No, that's all. Thanks Yosuke.

Y: No, thank you, and I'll get that quote for you this afternoon. Bye.

Notes

Unit 10 Trade Show

● VOCABULARY

Match the words with the meanings below

1) Attend	a) Fair, not too much
2) Register	b) Leave a hotel
3) Have you...	c) Join or go to an event
4) No problem	d) A good idea
5) Exhibit	e) The price of something
6) Samples	f) Did you do yet
7) Prepare	g) I can do that
8) Charge	h) Small examples of a product
9) Reasonable	i) Get ready for something
10) Check out	j) Make a promise to go to an event
11) Sounds good	k) Show your products

LISTENING PRACTICE

In this dialogue, Nori speaks with Yosuke from the Nissui Transportation Company about a container for frozen scallops. Listen to the dialogue once, and then answer the questions. After finishing the questions, check your answers. Listen to the dialogue a second time to check your answers one more time.

Questions for Dialogue 10: Trade Show

1. Where is the trade show that Sato san wants to attend?

☐ Dubai ☐ Boston ☐ Bombay ☐ Brussels

2. Which booth size is NOT available in Brussels?

☐ 3m² ☐ 6m² ☐ 10m² ☐ 15m²

3. Which size booth does Sato san want to reserve?

☐ 3m² ☐ 6m² ☐ 10m² ☐ 15m²

4. Will the company bring samples to the show?

☐ No, it won't ☐ No, I won't ☐ No, he won't ☐ I don't know

5. When is the expo?

☐ April ☐ May ☐ June ☐ July

6. How many nights will Nori and Sato san stay?

☐ By airplane ☐ No samples ☐ w3 ☐ Europe

7. Which advertising company will Nori contact?

☐ Dentsu ☐ Hakuhodo ☐ Asatsu ☐ Asahi

8. What will the advertising company make?

☐ Price offers ☐ Samples ☐ Brochures ☐ The booth

9. What is the name of the hotel they might stay at?

☐ Hilton ☐ Fairmont ☐ MAS ☐ Thon

10 When will Nori start preparing for the seafood expo?

☐ Tomorrow ☐ Now ☐ In a while ☐ After lunch

DISCUSSION TOPICS

1. Why are expos important for businesses?

_____

2. How many trade shows have you attended in your life?

_____

3. At some trade shows, companies use translators. Is this a good idea?

_____

4. What do you think people at trade shows do at night?

_____

5. Which seafood expo would you like to attend: Boston, Brussels, or Hong Kong?

_____

6. What is good and bad about bringing samples to a trade show?

_____

7. What would you do to prepare for a trade show in a foreign country?

_____

8. What is the nicest hotel you have stayed at in your life?

_____

USEFUL INFORMATION: At the Seafood Expo in Brussels, Organizers Ask Not To Forget...

- Passport, visa, flight tickets
- Hotel reservation confirmation and address
- Expo's address, hall, stand number, stand telephone numbers
- Full contact details of embassy/ Consulate of your country in Belgium
- Notification of Acceptance issued by CBI you got from us
- Business cards, company brochure/ catalogues, product samples info about packaging, production, and delivery
- List of customers you want to visit
- Contract which can be completed during conversation with customers during the fair
- Some pens, blank papers, calculator
- Laptop, laptop lock, European power connector
- Personal things, credit card, some cash
- List with contact details in case of emergency.

READING - Seafood Expo Blog

In 2013, the presidents of some of the biggest seafood suppliers from Hokkaido, Japan attended the Seafood Expo in Boston. It was an expo I will never forget for a few reasons.

We all met in Narita Airport, shaking hands and exchanging business cards. I was the only non-Japanese person in the group, and my English skills became <u>useful</u> very soon.

It is a long flight from Tokyo to Boston. But on this day, it was much, much longer. A snow storm was hitting Boston...in March. So, our plane landed in New York, and we were told to wait. So, we waited and waited until finally we were told, "Your flight is cancelled." But this was a group of presidents. They did not like this news. So, we made a new plan. Some people flew to Florida then Boston, some to Washington then Boston, and some just waited in New York. I stayed in New York.

We were 4 people, and at that time, my Japanese was poor (it is still poor). We ate, and drank, and drank some more. We checked the weather, checking for any flights to Boston. It was getting late, about 10pm, and people in the group were getting tired. And I was getting tired, too. Finally, we got good news. There was a flight to Boston leaving in 20 minutes. But we had to go to another part of the airport, and fast.

We all went to the gate in time. We arrived in Boston, and met everybody who went in different directions. When we got to the hotel, we were traveling for 26 hours. That was a long day.

At the expo, our booth was extremely busy. In Japan, Hokkaido seafood has a very strong reputation. Buyers from around the world asked questions. They sampled our sushi, and discussed business...all done in English.

For international business, having strong English language skills is very important. It helps connect people, and it builds trust and friendship that is essential to do any business.

During the trip, I helped negotiate business deals. I helped guide our group to the right gate. I made restaurant reservations. I helped show foreign buyers that our company can do business with them easily. And this was because I can speak English.

READING COMPREHENSION

1. Why was the flight to Boston so long?

_____

2. Who went to Boston?

_____

3. Why is it important to have strong English language skills?

_____

4. What is the reputation of Hokkaido seafood?

_____

5. If you went to Boston, would you want a translator? Why or why not?

_____

GRAMMAR PRACTICE - Present Perfect Tense

This verb tense uses HAVE + past participle (過去分詞) of a verb. For example,

> **I *HAVE LIVED* in Hawaii for 3 years.**

In the past, the person moved to Hawaii, and the person **STILL** lives in Hawaii. How long? For 3 years. If the person DOES NOT live in Hawaii now, we can write:

> **I *LIVED* in Hawaii for 3 years** (but NOT NOW).

Using **SINCE** & **FOR**

> **FOR- a long time, 2 years, 2 weeks, 5 days...**
> **SINCE - 9pm, Monday, I was young, March, 2014...**

As you can see, SINCE is used in many ways. FOR usually uses a number, and is a little easier to use.

PRACTICE—Answer the questions. Be careful to use the correct verb tense.

1. How long have you <u>lived</u> in this city?

_____

2. How long have you <u>had</u> your pencil?

_____

3. How long have you <u>studied</u> English?

_____

4. How long have you <u>drunk</u> alcohol?

_____

5. How long have you <u>driven</u> a car?

_____

6. How long have you been studying English today?

_____

WRITING PRACTICE - Making a Brochure

Every company is different, so when making a brochure, it is important to know what information you need to include. Complete the brochure below, writing about the 7 parts below (see **page 93** for an example):

1. Company name
2. Contact information (i.e. Company name and email addresses)
3. Product name
4. Info about product and preparation (i.e. Best ways to eat the product)
5. Catch season & area
6. Defrosting methods
7. Taste

① ②

③

③

④ ④

⑤ ⑥ ⑦

Answer Key and Notes Unit 10

Vocabulary (p. 86)

1. C   2. J   3. F   4. G   5. K   6. H   7. I   8. E   9. A   10. B

Listening (p. 87)

1. Brussels   2. $10m^2$ 3. $3m^2$ 4. No, it won't   5. April
6. 3   7. Dentsu   8. Brochures   9. MAS   10. Now

Reading (p. 89)

1. The trip was long because a snow storm delayed the flight.

2. The presidents of some of the biggest seafood companies in Hokkaido.

3. Strong language skills help connect people, building trust and friendship that is essential to do any business.

4. Hokkaido's seafood reputation is very good in Japan and around the world.

5. Yes, I would because then I could have less stress communicating with people.

Grammar (p. 90) - *Answers can use either FOR or SINCE*

1. I have lived in this city FOR 3 years.

2. I have had my pencil for 2 months.

3. I have studied English since high school (OR since I was in high school)

4. I don't drink alcohol.

5. I have driven a car since I was 18 yearsold.

6. I have been studying for 1 hour.

Writing (p. 91)

1. <u>Company name</u> - 丸水札幌中央水株式会社 / Marusui Sapporo Chuo Suisan

2. <u>Contact information</u> (i.e. Names and email addresses) - Norihito Suzuki / n-suzuki@marusui net.co.jp

3. <u>Product name and information about the product</u> - Hotate / The Product
Scallops from Hokkaido are all natural, chemical-free, famous for their freshness, high- quality with
low water content. These scallops are favoured by sushi chefs for their top dishes.

4. <u>Preparation</u> (i.e. Best ways to eat the product) - At the recent World Gourmet Series Awards of Excellence chefs used braised Hokkaido scallops with winter melon. In Japan, top sushi chefs prefer them raw for live scallop sashimi.

5. <u>Catch season & area</u> - Hotate are caught in the Okhotsk Sea from June-November, and in the Nemuro area from January-May.

6. <u>Defrosting methods</u> - To get the best taste, defrost the scallops in the fridge overnight. If needed, place the scallops in a bowl under a running tap for about 15 minutes.

7. <u>Taste</u> - Hokkaido hotate have a tender, exquisite taste, taking up to 4 years in waters rich in nutrients carried from the Arctic Ocean to reach a fresh, extremely delicious taste.

Dialogue - Trade Shows

Sato san: Nori, we will attend the Seafood Expo in Brussels this year.
Nori: Have you registered yet?

Sato: No, I haven't, so I want you to do that today.
Nori: No problem. I'll start right away.

———————————————— 20 minutes later ————————————————

Nori: Sato san, I have a few questions for you. First. What size booth do you want? $3m^2$, $6m^2$, or $15m^2$?

Sato; We will exhibit alone this year, so $3m^2$ is fine.
Nori: Okay. What kind of products will we bring to the expo? Samples, brochures, offer sheets...

Sato: No samples, but we need to prepare brochures.
Nori: Do you want to use the ones we already have, or hire a professional company to design them?

Sato: Find out how much a company would charge to design them.
Nori: I'll call my friend at Dentsu Advertising. We can save some money on hotel rooms. Last year we stayed at the Hotel MAS, and the price was reasonable. How many nights will we stay?

Sato: Reserve 3 nights. The expo is from April 21-23. So we can arrive on the 20th, check out on the 23rd, and come home after the show.
Nori: Sounds good. I'll get right on it.

Appendix

Companies make brochures for many reasons. Some companies want to focus on the image of the product, especially if the buyers may not know about the product. Other companies might want to focus on information about the product, such as catch area and time.

Whatever the reason, all brochures need to be planned and well-designed to promote the selling idea.

On the following pages, there are a few examples of brochures for different seafood products. These brochures were done using Microsoft Word or Microsoft Publisher. Many times, I was asked to make the brochure using Excel. This is because it is very easy to change information in this program.

This becomes important when other people in the company use the brochure, but do not know how to make changes without altering the design of the brochure.

Sake

MARUSUI SAPPORO

CHUO SUISAN CO., INC.

http://www.marusui-net.co.jp

n-suzuki@marusui-net.co.jp

SALMON FROM HOKKAIDO

VARIETIES

Chum Salmon dominates the catch in Hokkaido. There are several types and brands of chum salmon caught in Hokkaido: *tokishirazu* (prized for its rich oil content), *ginsei* (famous for its shiny silver color), *keiji* (20-30% fat throughout its body), and *mejika* (famous for its soft, round body). As well as chum salmon, pink, masu, Chinook, coho, and sockeye are all caught around Hokkaido.

CATCH SIZE AND AREA

There are 3 types of salmon caught in Hokkaido with catch sizes over 100t. Hokkaido accounts for 82% of the entire salmon catch in Japan. Chum salmon dominates the catch (128 441t in 2010, 110 000 in 2011), followed by pink salmon (10 254t), and masu salmon (763t).

Chum salmon is caught in 5 main areas in Hokkaido.

The largest catch is in the Okhotsk Sea, followed by the Nemuro Straight, the East Pacific, the West Pacific, and the Japan Sea. The catch sizes in these areas

TASTE AND HEALTH

Since most chum salmon spawns near river mouths, they have lower oil content than sockeye, Chinook, or coho. For sushi, lower fat content can be more delicious where other fatty types of salmon can be unappetizing due to an over-abundance of fat.

Chum salmon has a mild taste, is low in sodium, and is a good source of omega-3 fatty acids, niacin, vitamin B12, and selenium. In many ways, it can be seen as the salmon best suited for health-conscious consumers.

ACCOLADES

Chum salmon has been described as "the best value on the market when the skin is bright and the meat deep red" (seafoodchoices). Chef Nakamura (Shangri-La Hotel, Taipei) described the *tokishirazu* chum salmon as "precious" for its "plumpness and tender sweet meat."

The *ginsei* chum salmon had the honor of being selected as the first ingredient to be used in the new Iron Chef Japan on October 26, 2012.

As for *mejika* chum salmon, it was described by one food critic as "outrageously delicious...far and away the finest piece of salmon I have ever tasted."

HISTORY

Commercial fishing for salmon began in the 19th century in Hokkaido. As stocks were over-fished, the need to establish salmon hatcheries was created. The first salmon hatchery was built in Chitose, Hokkaido in 1889. Currently, approximately 1 billion chum and 150 million pink juvenile salmon are released each year in Hokkaido rivers. Chum salmon is the largest salmon species caught in Hokkaido, accounting for about 10% of the entire Hokkaido catch, and is the largest

Grilled Thai salmon

Ingredients

4 x 140g/5oz salmon fillets

2 tsp sunflower oil

small knob of root ginger, peeled and grated

1 mild red chilli, finely sliced (deseed if you want less heat)

bunch spring onions, finely sliced

1½ tbsp sweet soy sauce

¼ tsp sugar

1 x 20g pack coriander, leaves only chopped

Cooking method

Heat grill to high. Place the fish in a shallow baking dish, then grill for 4-5 mins until cooked through, but still a little pink in the centre. Cover and set aside.

Heat a wok, add the oil, then stir-fry the ginger, chilli and spring onions for 2-3 mins. Stir in the soy, sugar and a splash of water, then take off the heat. Throw in the coriander and serve immediately with the salmon. Delicious with

丸水札幌中央水株式会社
Marusui Sapporo Chuo Suisan

www.marusui-net.co.jp
s-gomi@marusui-net.co.jp

Alaska Pollock
スケトウダラ

Features of Hokkaido Alaska Pollock

Product

Alaska pollock roe is processed into either tarako (called cod roe) or mentaiko (spicy cod roe). Mentaiko is famous for its spicy-salty taste that leaves a fresh taste of the sea in your mouth. Tarako has a sweet-salty taste, used in many dishes.

Hokkaido processors remove the roe from the Alaska pollock before freezing the fish. When processed on board, the roe is removed and quickly frozen to ensure an excellent texture of the grain.

Preparation

With hundreds of producers scattered around Hokkaido and Japan, the taste of Alaska pollock roe varies from company to company. Either soaked in a salt brine or in chilli flakes, sake and secret ingredients, tarako and mentaiko can be served in a number of ways:

Plain (usually for breakfast)

As a filling for rice balls (*onigiri*)

As a pasta sauce (usually with *nori*)

Catch Season and Area

In Japan, Alaska pollock is caught mainly in the Sea of Japan from October to March. The roe is best when processed in fall and winter. Outside of Japan, Russia is the main supplier to Hokkaido processors.

Defrosting

Alaska pollock roe is a raw food, so it is best eaten fresh, not frozen. However, when freezing, wrap the pieces individually, and thaw them slowly in your fridge the night before you plan to use them.

Taste

Mentaiko has a crunchy, grainy texture, spicy to the tongue that leaves a mild sweet and salty seafood flavour. Tarako has a similar texture, with a fresh, seafood taste that is between sweet and salty